NATURE'S
contemporary knitted shawls
WRAPTURE

Sheryl Thies

Martingale®
& COMPANY

DEDICATION

For Ellie

ACKNOWLEDGMENTS

Thanks to all my knitting friends for your suggestions, which helped me to refine my ideas.

Thanks to Martingale & Company for the opportunity to publish and to all of the staff who diligently worked to transform my manuscript into this book. A special thanks to my technical editor, Robin Strobel.

Thanks to my husband, Kevin, for your encouragement and enthusiasm.

Nature's Wrapture:
Contemporary Knitted Shawls
© 2010 by Sheryl Thies

Martingale
& C O M P A N Y

Martingale & Company
20205 144th Ave. NE
Woodinville, WA 98072-8478 USA
www.martingale-pub.com

Printed in China
15 14 13 12 11 10   8 7 6 5 4 3 2 1

Library of Congress Cataloging-in-Publication Data is available upon request

ISBN: 978-1-56477-944-1

credits

President & CEO: Tom Wierzbicki
Editor in Chief: Mary V. Green
Managing Editor: Tina Cook
Developmental Editor: Karen Costello Soltys
Technical Editor: Robin Strobel
Copy Editor: Liz McGehee
Design Director: Stan Green
Production Manager: Regina Girard
Illustrator: Laurel Strand
Cover & Text Designer: Shelly Garrison
Photographer: Brent Kane

mission statement

Dedicated to providing quality products and service to inspire creativity.

CONTENTS

CREATIVE EVOLUTION

This collection of wraps is the culmination of events that spanned several decades. On a sunny Sunday afternoon in early fall more than twenty years ago, my neighbor Ellie and I went for a walk. Since then, our daily walk became our preferred form of exercise and when one of us wasn't motivated to venture outdoors, the other would coax and cajole until we were both out pounding the pavement.

Our route and distance varied, depending on the weather and season. We took full advantage of the nature trails, parks, and bike trails in the area and occasionally ventured into the nearby arboretum. We watched leaves on trees turn from green to incredible shades of yellow, red, and bronze and finally drop to the ground, where we could rustle through the piles in the street. Butterflies fluttered across our path, bumblebees buzzed by our heads, and dragonflies hovered and danced before us.

We quickened our pace as sheets of rain approached and sometimes made it home without getting wet. We took pleasure as we watched the sun set and twilight magically suffused the neighborhood, the first stars appearing in the night sky.

On a cross-country tromp through the woods, the path gave way to underbrush and briars so thick we could not take another step. But there at our fingertips were plump, lush raspberries hanging heavy on their thorny, prickly stems. This course became our July favorite.

Winter was a little less idyllic. After the enchantment of the first snowfall gave way to plummeting temperatures and shoulder-high mounds of drifted snow, walking became more of an act of courage than an enjoyable form of exercise. Two consecutive winters of record snowfall, more than 100 inches, made us reconsider venturing outdoors. Temporarily reneging on our exercise plan seemed a prudent choice.

While waiting for the snow and temperature to stop falling, I had time to knit and watch the flames dance in the fireplace. It was then that I realized nature could be knit, and the concept for this book began to form.

A WALK THROUGH NATURE

Mantles, capes, and cloaks—loose, sleeveless outer garments worn over other clothes—are part of historical dress. George Washington wore a cape as he crossed the Delaware River for the surprise attack on Trenton. Clara Barton's cape became a symbol of the nursing profession, and Clint Eastwood's "Spaghetti Poncho" was considered a standard of western gear.

No longer considered vintage, wraps of various types and shapes are worn for style over fancy dresses, relaxed jeans, and even beachwear. Not just for warmth, wraps span the seasons and the climates. A versatile wrap can grace your shoulders and double as a ground cover (when the only place to sit is on the ground) or as an afghan for a sleeping toddler.

Nature's Wrapture incorporates fascinating aspects of nature—colors, contours, textures, and patterns—with classic and updated shapes that flatter all body types, resulting in a real sense of inspired style. Interesting to knit and simple to wear, the adapted shapes hug the shoulders and are easy to keep in place while leading an active lifestyle.

From the elegant and sublime to the practical, this collection has broad appeal not only for the knitter but also for the wearer. Extroverts will pirouette and swirl wearing Sunset, cheer with delight wearing Butterflies, flutter at the sight of Dragonfly, and buzz friends with Bumblebees. The more subtle will appreciate the beauty of Roses, the delicate structure of Orchids, and the drops of Heavy Rain tipped with a picot of beads. Fun-loving people of all ages will applaud at the sight of Raspberries and express wonder at Supernova and Milky Way. Those seeking comfort will be soothed with the luxury of Sandy Beach, protected by Cocoon, and warmed by Flames.

Be creative when wearing these flattering wraps. Remember, they can be draped over the shoulders, worn backwards with ends hanging down the back, or hung on one shoulder and cinched with a belt at the waist. They can be tied, knotted, closed with pins and rings from your jewelry box, or held in place with shawl pins, clasps, and buttons. In the grip of winter weather, position a wrap over your winter coat to add another layer of warmth and to brighten drab coat colors.

Nature's Wrapture is complete with all the information needed to create the wraps. But don't stop there; feel free to change colors, simplify patterns, or add detail. Express your own interpretation of nature by adding personal touches for a one-of-a-kind wrap. Your creations will be worn and treasured for years to come.

BEFORE CASTING ON

Texture, patterns, and colors dominate the projects in this collection of nature-inspired wraps. The techniques used—lace, simple yarn-over patterns, twist and crossover stitches, and fancy ribbings—may be new to you, but that doesn't make them hard to master. Often the pattern is repetitive and the repeat is easily memorized.

SKILL LEVEL

The Craft Yarn Council of America developed guidelines for determining skill levels that may help guide you to a project within your expertise. The skill levels for all of these wraps are either beginner, easy, or intermediate. Wraps are generally uncomplicated to work due to their simple silhouettes with little or no shaping, minimal finishing, and the relatively small number of stitches in a row. If you know how to cast on, knit, purl, and bind off, and the wrap appeals to you, give it a try. A little practice of the specific stitch pattern or technique should be enough to build your skill level so that you can successfully complete the project.

◼◻◻◻ **Beginner:** Projects for first-time knitters using basic knit and purl stitches. Minimal shaping.

◼◼◻◻ **Easy:** Projects using basic stitches, repetitive stitch patterns, and simple color changes. Simple shaping and finishing.

◼◼◼◻ **Intermediate:** Projects using a variety of stitches, such as basic cables and lace, simple intarsia, techniques for double-pointed needles, and knitting in the round. Mid-level shaping and finishing.

◼◼◼◼ **Experienced:** Projects using advanced techniques and stitches, such as short rows, Fair Isle, intricate intarsia, cables, lace patterns, and numerous color changes.

YARN

Start by visiting your local yarn store to select that perfect yarn. If you want your completed project to look like the one in the book, choose the same yarn or one with similar gauge, fiber, and structure. If you choose a yarn that is markedly different, understand that the end product will be markedly different—although it may still result in a very attractive and striking garment. The choice is yours.

Some of the unknowns of selecting and substituting yarn can be reduced by reading the yarn label. The label will state the needle size and gauge, yardage, fiber content, and care instructions. When substituting yarn, pick a yarn that is a similar weight (thickness). To make this selection easier, there are universal symbols indicating yarn weights. The weight of the yarn used for each project is indicated with a corresponding symbol. Comparing the yarn-weight symbol to the Standard Yarn Weights chart on page 79 will identify the type of yarn you should be looking for.

Be sure to purchase a sufficient amount of yarn. The directions, under the heading of "Materials," give the number of skeins for each project and the yardage for each skein. Multiply the number of balls times the amount of yarn on each ball to determine the total number of yards required for the specific wrap. Once you find a yarn that you would like to use, read the label to determine the yardage for that skein. Divide the total number of yards required by the amount in each ball of the substituted yarn to determine the number of balls you should purchase. Sometimes you will have some yarn left over; this is a lot better than running short. If you've ever run short and were unable to purchase enough yarn to complete the project, you understand the importance of purchasing enough. Also, if you want to alter the project—make it larger or longer—remember to purchase more yarn.

GAUGE SWATCH

Don't overlook the importance of gauge. The gauge given for each project may not seem to correspond to the gauge suggested on the yarn label. The stitch pattern greatly affects the number of stitches per inch. The only way to know if you have the right combination of yarn and needles is to make a gauge swatch—and in some cases, make another and another swatch until the gauge is correct.

The gauge swatch is the perfect way to master the stitch pattern. To make a gauge swatch in a pattern stitch, you want to end up with a knit piece about 4" square. The gauge given as part of the instructions will indicate the number of stitches for 4", but check the pattern-stitch multiple number. For example, if the multiple is nine plus four, cast on 22 stitches (9 stitches x 2 repeats + 4 edge stitches = 22 stitches). This will allow you to work two complete pattern

repeats. Work in the pattern until the piece measures 4", or longer if there are more rows to the pattern. Measure the width of the swatch and divide by 22 stitches to calculate the number of stitches per inch. If the number of stitches per inch is less then the desired number, go down a needle size and repeat the pattern. If the number of stitches per inch is more than the desired number, go up a needle size.

All gauges for the projects are given after blocking using the stated blocking method. Stitch patterns before blocking often bunch together and hide the beauty of the pattern. Blocking will open up, spread and even out the stitches, and give the proper dimensions to the finished piece. Amazingly, a blocked piece of lace looks completely different than the unblocked piece. Several different methods for blocking are discussed on page 77, and each project specifies a suggested blocking method.

You may have to repeat this process several times to get to the stated stitch gauge. You may feel this is a waste of time. However, if you want the project to turn out as described, the proper gauge needs to be achieved. If you want to freelance and try something different, go for it; you may end up with a greatly enhanced and

desirable piece of work. But if you want it to look like the photo and it doesn't, gauge is probably the culprit.

The good news with gauge is that generally you don't have to deal with row gauge. Since all but one of the patterns are written in inches, rather than rows per inch, row gauge is not even specified in the patterns. The Roses wrap is the only project with a stated row gauge.

Before going on to the actual project, you may want to work a few more pattern repeats to become more familiar with the techniques used in the pattern stitch. The exact execution of a step will impact the outcome of a piece. For example, a M1 (make one stitch) and a YO (yarn over the needle) are two ways of increasing one stitch; however, there is a big difference in the result. The M1 is an almost invisible increase, while the YO is an increase that leaves a very noticeable hole.

Several projects have a crocheted edge rather than a knit edge. The various trims provide a decorative finish and stabilize the edges. For more information, see the "Techniques" section on page 74. Even for a novice, the trims can be completed easily and quickly. Use your gauge swatch to practice the edgings.

BUMBLEBEES

Bumblebees feed on the nectar of flowers, and they fulfill the important role of pollinators for both crops and wildflowers. Since its stinger is not barbed, the bumblebee is capable of stinging more than once. Wear this bumblebee wrap with an uneven edge and I-cord ties and you will be the queen bee.

SKILL LEVEL

Intermediate ◼◼◼▢

FINISHED MEASUREMENTS

Width at top edge: 47"

Length at longest point: 18"

MATERIALS

2 skeins of Euroflax Fine/Sport Weight from Louet (100% wet spun linen; 100 g/3.5 oz; 270 yds) in color Terra Cotta 18-2474-11 🧶②

US 5 (3.75 mm) circular needle (24") or size required to obtain gauge

US 5 (3.75 mm) double-pointed needles

Size 8 (5 mm) needles

Size G (4 mm) crochet hook

GAUGE

18 sts = 4" in patt st when blocked

STITCH PATTERN

bumblebees

(Multiple of 8 + 2)

Chart on page 10.

Row 1 (RS): K2, *K1, K2tog, YO twice, ssk, K3, rep from *.

Row 2 and all WS rows: Purl, working K1, P1 into every double YO.

Row 3: K2, *K2tog, K1, YO twice, K1, ssk, K2, rep from *.

Row 5: K1, K2tog, *K2, YO twice, K2, ssk, K2tog, rep from* to last 7 sts, K2, YO twice, K2, ssk, K1.

Row 7: K1, YO, *ssk, K4, K2tog, YO twice, rep from * to last 9 sts, ssk, K4, K2tog, YO, K1.

Row 9: K1, YO, *K1, ssk, K2, K2tog, K1, YO twice, rep from * to last 9 sts, K1, ssk, K2, K2tog, K1, YO, K1.

Row 11: K1, YO, *K2, ssk, K2tog, K2, YO twice, rep from * to last 9 sts, K2, ssk, K2tog, K2, YO, K1.

Row 12: Purl, working K1, P1 into every double YO.

Rep rows 1–12 for patt.

WRAP

With circular needle, CO 146 sts. Purl 1 row and work 22 rows in bumblebees patt. Inc as follows: At end of row 10, CO 16 sts using backward-loop method (see page 74). Turn work. K16 and cont across row 11 in established patt. CO 16 sts before turning work—178 sts. Cont in bumblebees patt for 22 more rows. Rep inc as above—210 sts. Cont in patt until piece measures approximately 18" when slightly stretched, ending with row 12. Knit 1 row. Purl 1 row. Using larger needles, BO all sts loosely.

FINISHING

With circular needle, PU 210 sts across top edge and set work aside.

Work I-cord for 12" or desired length as follows: With dpn, CO 4 sts. *K4. Without turning work, slide sts to other end of needle, pull yarn tightly across the back of sts, and rep from *. Join and work applied I-cord across 210 sts along top edge of wrap as follows: **K3 sts from dpn, work ssk with last st on dpn and first PU st on circular needle. Sl 4 sts from dpn to unused end of circular needle and rep from ** until all PU sts are bound off. Using dpns, cont to work 12" of I-cord. BO 4 sts.

With RS facing you and crochet hook, sc along all side edges, across bottom edge, and along second side, working 3 sc sts in each outer corner. Break yarn. Weave in all ends. Block using wet blocking method (see page 77).

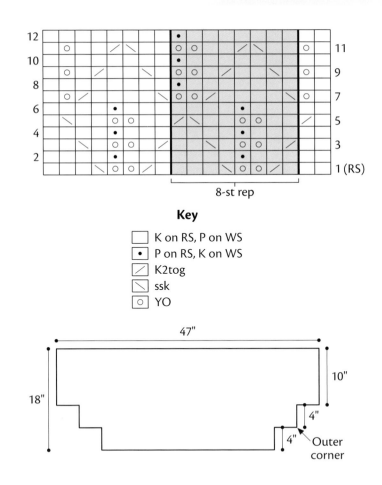

8-st rep

Key

- ☐ K on RS, P on WS
- ▪ P on RS, K on WS
- ⟋ K2tog
- ⟍ ssk
- ○ YO

CHUNKY BAMBOO

In many cultures, bamboo is thought to bring luck, longevity, and good fortune. Create your own beautiful bamboo with this reversible pattern of chunky bamboo ribbing, complete with self-finished edge and armhole slit. May it bring you luck, longevity, and good fortune.

SKILL LEVEL

Beginner ■□□□

FINISHED MEASUREMENTS

Width: 53"

Length: 20½"

MATERIALS

10 skeins of Aster Magic from Universal Yarn (56% polyamid, 26% viscose, 18% Dralon; 50 g/1.76 oz; 98 yds) in color 9103 ③

US 7 (4.5 mm) needles or size required to obtain gauge

Purchased shawl pin (optional)

GAUGE

20 sts = 4" in patt, slightly stretched

STITCH PATTERN

chunky-bamboo ribbing

(Multiple of 6 + 8)

Chart on page 13.

Rows 1, 3, 5, and 7 (RS): K6, *P2, K4, rep from * to last 2 sts, sl 2 wyib.

Rows 2, 4, 6, and 8: P6, *K2, P4, rep from * to last 2 sts, sl 2 wyif.

Row 9: K2, P4, *K2, P4, rep from * to last 2 sts, sl 2 wyib.

Row 10: P2, K4, *P2, K4, rep from * to last 2 sts, sl 2 wyif.

Rep rows 1 – 10 for patt.

WRAP

CO 104 sts and work in chunky-bamboo-ribbing patt until piece measures 13", ending with row 2. Shape armhole slit as follows: Work row 3 of patt across 40 sts, BO next 24 sts in patt, cont in patt across last 40 sts. Work row 4 of patt across 40 sts, CO 24 sts using cable CO (see page 74), cont across last 40 sts in patt. Resume patt with row 5 and cont until piece measures 53", ending with row 8. BO all sts loosely in patt.

CHUNKY BAMBOO

FINISHING

Weave in all ends. Block using damp-towel method (see page 77).

SHERYL'S NOTES

Wear with the slit low on the forearm or high above the elbow. Close with a purchased shawl pin or wear without a pin. To eliminate the armhole slit, work across rows three and four without binding off or casting on.

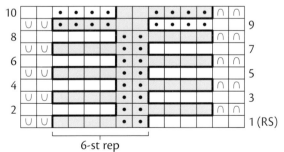

6-st rep

Key

	K on RS, P on WS
•	P on RS, K on WS
∪	sl 1 wyib
∩	sl 1 wyif

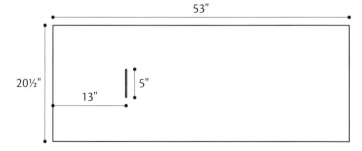

BUTTERFLIES

Butterflies attract attention with their brightly colored wings and graceful flight. Enjoy being the center of attention wearing this lace-weight wrap with slip-stitch butterflies, two-color crochet edge, and Hana Silk Ribbon.

SKILL LEVEL

Intermediate ■■■□

FINISHED MEASUREMENTS

Width without crochet edge: 56"

Length without crochet edge: 24½"

MATERIALS

Lace from Malabrigo Yarn (100% baby merino wool; 50 g; 470 yds) [1]

A: 2 skeins of color 37 Lettuce

B: 2 skeins of color 55 Floral

US 6 (4 mm) needles or size required to obtain gauge

US G (4 mm) crochet hook

1 yd Hana Silk Ribbon, ⅝" wide, color China Doll (optional)

GAUGE

24 sts = 4" in patt after blocking

STITCH PATTERNS

butterfly

(Multiple of 16 + 3)

Chart on page 17.

Work with only 1 color of yarn in each row. Sl all sts as if to purl, holding yarn in back on RS rows and holding yarn in front on WS rows unless indicated otherwise.

Row 1 (RS): With B, K1, *K7, sl 1, K1, sl 1, K6, rep from * to last 2 sts, K2.

Row 2 and all WS rows: Purl sts worked on previous row with same-color yarn, sl all sl sts from previous row.

Row 3: With A, K1, *(sl 1, K1) 4 times, K8, rep from * to last 2 sts, sl 1, K1.

Row 5: With B, K1, *K7, sl 1, K3, (sl 1, K1) twice, sl 1, rep from * to last 2 sts, K2.

Row 7: With A, K1, *(sl 1, K1) 3 times, K2, (sl 1, K1) twice, K4, rep from * to last 2 sts, sl 1, K1.

Row 9: With B, K1, *K5, sl 1, K1, sl 1, K5, sl 1, K1, sl 1, rep from * to last 2 sts, K2.

Row 11: With A, K1, *(sl 1, K1) twice, K4, (sl 1, K1) 3 times, K2, rep from * to last 2 sts, sl 1, K1.

BUTTERFLIES

Row 13: With B, K1, *K3, (sl 1, K1) 3 times, K6, sl 1, rep from * to last 2 sts, K2.

Row 15: With A, K1, *K8, (sl 1, K1) 4 times, rep from * to last 2 sts, K2.

Row 17: With B, K1, *K1, sl 1, K13, sl 1, rep from * to last 2 sts, K2.

Row 19: With A, K1, *K2, (sl 1, K1) 4 times, K6, rep from * to last 2 sts, K2.

Row 21: With B, K1, *K1, sl 1, K7, (sl 1, K1) 3 times, K1, rep from * to last 2 sts, K2.

Row 23: With A, K1, *sl 1, K3, (sl 1, K1) 3 times, K4, sl 1, K1, rep from * to last 2 sts, sl 1, K1.

Row 25: With B, K1, *K1, (sl 1, K1) twice, K4, (sl 1, K1) twice, K3, rep from * to last 2 sts, K2.

Row 27: With A, K1, *sl 1, K5, (sl 1, K1) twice, K2, (sl 1, K1) twice, rep from * to last 2 sts, sl 1, K1.

Row 29: With B, K1, *(K1, sl 1) 3 times, K3, sl 1, K6, rep from * to last 2 sts, K2.

Row 31: With A, K1, *sl 1, K9, (sl 1, K1) 3 times, rep from * to last 2 sts, sl 1, K1.

Row 32: With A, purl the sts worked on previous row, sl all sl sts on previous row.

Rep rows 1–32 for patt.

2-color crocheted cable edge

Rnd 1: With A, sc around all edges, working 2 sc in each corner. Sl st to join.

Rnd 2: With A, ch 3, work 1 dc, *ch 3, skip 2 sts, work 1 dc, rep from * around all edges. Sl st to join.

Rnd 3: With B, ch 3, work 1 dc, *ch 3, take hook out of last ch, insert under ch-3 loop of previous row, place last ch back on hook, and draw through loop; rep from * around all edges, sl st to join and fasten off.

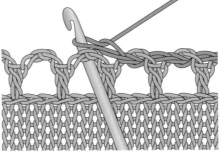

Take hook out of last ch, insert under ch-3 loop of previous row, and draw through loop.

WRAP

With A, CO 147 sts and purl 1 row. Beg butterfly patt and work until piece measures about 56", ending with row 32. With A, knit 1 row. BO all sts pw.

FINISHING

Weave in all ends. Block using wet method (see page 77).

With RS facing you and crochet hook, beg in corner and work 2-color crocheted cable edge along all sides of wrap. Weave 18" piece of Hana Silk Ribbon through crocheted edge along short side of wrap and gather slightly to form cuff. Knot and trim ends to desired length.

SHERYL'S NOTES

The silk-ribbon cuff is optional. Wear this wrap as a shawl and, if desired, close with a shawl pin.

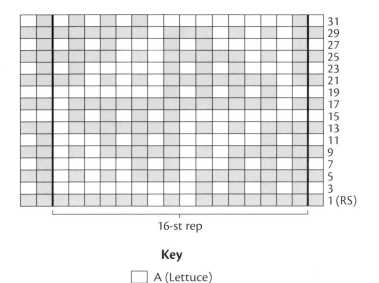

31
29
27
25
23
21
19
17
15
13
11
9
7
5
3
1 (RS)

16-st rep

Key

☐ A (Lettuce)
▨ B (Floral)

- Work each row with only 1 yarn color. The first edge st indicates working color. For other color, with yarn at back, sl 1 st.
- Sl all sts as if to purl.
- Chart shows only odd-numbered (RS) rows. On even-numbered (WS) rows, with same working color as previous row, purl all purl sts as they face you, and with yarn at front, sl all the slipped sts from previous row.

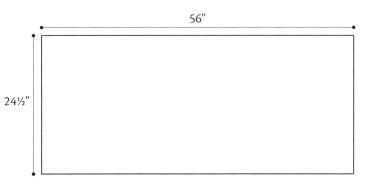

56"

24½"

COCOON

The silky envelope that forms around a larva provides protection while the caterpillar undergoes transformation. Slip this fantastically textured cocoon over your head and experience your own transformation.

SKILL LEVEL

Easy ◼◼☐☐

FINISHED MEASUREMENTS

Small/Medium (Large/Extra Large)

Width: 47 (51)"

Length with collar turned down: 17 (18)"

MATERIALS

8 (9) skeins of Royal Llama Silk from Plymouth Yarn Company (60% fine llama, 40% silk; 50 g; 102 yds) in color 1829 ⓸

US 9 (5.5 mm) needles or size required to obtain gauge

US 8 (5 mm) needles

US 10 (6 mm) needles

Tapestry needle

Safety pin (optional)

GAUGE

18 sts = 4" in patt, slightly stretched, with size 9 needles

STITCH PATTERN

COCOON

(Multiple of 8 + 3)

Chart on page 20.

Row 1 (RS): K2, *P5, K1, P1, K1, rep from * to last st, K1.

Row 2: P2, *M1, (K1, P1, K1) in next st, M1, P1, P5tog, P1, rep from * to last st, K1.

Rows 3, 5, and 7: K2, *P1, K1, P5, K1, rep from * to last st, P1.

Rows 4 and 6: P2, *K5, P1, K1, P1, rep from * to last st, K1.

Row 8: P2, *P5 tog, P1, M1, (K1, P1, K1) in next st, M1, P1, rep from * to last st, P1.

Rows 9 and 11: K2, *P5, K1, P1, K1, rep from * to last st, K1.

Rows 10 and 12: P2, *K1, P1, K5, P1, rep from * to last st, P1.

Rep rows 1–12 for patt.

WRAP

With size 9 needles, CO 211 (227) sts. Purl 1 row, knit 1 row, purl 1 row. Work setup row as follows: P2, *K1, P1, K5, P1, rep from * to last st, P1. Beg cocoon patt and cont in patt until piece measures 15 (16)", ending with row 1.

Change to size 8 needles and beg shoulder shaping. Dec 13 (14) sts as follows: P2, *K1, P1, K5, P1, K1, P1, ssk, K3, P1, rep

from * to last st, P1—198 (213) sts. Work 1 row in established patt, knitting the knit sts and purling the purl sts as they face you.

Dec 13 (14) sts as follows: P2, *K1, P1, ssk, K3, P1, K1, P1, K4, P1, rep from * to last st, P1—185 (199) sts. Work 1 row in established patt, knitting the knit sts and purling the purl sts as before.

Dec 26 (28) sts as follows: P2, *K1, P1, ssk, K2, P1, rep from * to last st, P1—159 (171) sts. Work 1 row in established patt.

Dec 26 (28) sts as follows: P2, *K1, P1, ssk, K1, P1, rep from * to last st, P1—133 (143) sts. Work 1 row in established patt.

Dec 26 (28) sts as follows: P2, *K1, P1, ssk, P1, rep from * to last st, P1—107 (115) sts. Mark row with safety pin for easier measuring.

Work in K1, P1 ribbing for 4". Change to size 9 needles and cont K1, P1 ribbing until ribbing measures 6". Change to size 10 needles and work until K1, P1 ribbing measures 7". BO all sts very loosely in patt.

FINISHING

Sew side edges as follows: Beg at bottom edge with RS facing out, sew seam to last 4". Turn wrap inside out and cont sewing last 4" of seam. Weave in ends. Turn collar outward. Block using mist method (see page 77). Wear with seam in back.

SHERYL'S NOTES

This wrap looks terrific on people of different sizes and shapes. If you prefer a longer version, work additional reps of the cocoon pattern before beg shoulder shaping. You will need to purchase additional yarn.

If you find P5tog too difficult, try using crochet hook to pull yarn through. You can also substitute sl 2 wyif-P3tog-p2sso for P5tog.

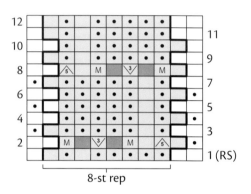

8-st rep

Key

☐	K on RS, P on WS
•	P on RS, K on WS
M	M1
↘3	K1, P1, K1 in 1 st
�ⁱ5	P5tog
▨	No st

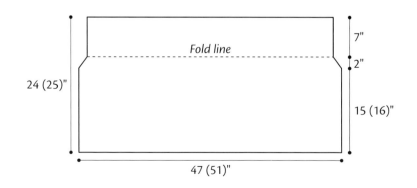

Fold line

7"

2"

24 (25)"

15 (16)"

47 (51)"

DRAGONFLY

With fluttering wings, the dragonfly floats just out of reach, then quickly flits off, alighting on a nearby leaf. No longer out of reach, the dragonflies on this wrap will spark your sense of freedom as they hover above the lacy leaf edging.

SKILL LEVEL

Intermediate ◼◼◼◻

FINISHED MEASUREMENTS

Width: 60"

Length: 17"

MATERIALS

8 skeins of Bonsai from Berroco (97% bamboo, 3% nylon; 50 g/1.75 oz; 77 yds) in color 4162 Haruna Green ⓸

Size 9 (5.5 mm) needles or size required to obtain gauge

Extra size 9 needles

4 stitch markers

Stitch holder

GAUGE

15 sts = 4" in St st

STITCH PATTERNS

edge stitch

Row 1: K3 sts, work leaf patt to last 3 sts, K1, sl 2 wyib.

Row 2: P3, work leaf patt to last 3 sts, P1, sl 2 wyif.

Work rows 1 and 2 for patt.

leaf

(Multiple of 19 + 20)

Chart on page 25.

Rows 1, 3, 5, 7, 9 (RS): K1, (YO, ssk) twice, YO, K3, K2tog, *ssk, K3, (YO, K2tog) twice, YO, K1, (YO, ssk) twice, YO, K3, K2tog, rep from * to last 10 sts, ssk, K3, (YO, K2tog) twice, YO, K1.

Row 2 and all WS rows: Purl.

Row 11: K2, (YO, ssk) twice, YO, K2, K2tog, *ssk, K2, YO, (K2tog, YO) twice, K3, (YO, ssk) twice, YO, K2, K2tog, rep from* to last 10 sts, ssk, K2, (YO, K2tog) twice, YO, K2.

Row 13: K3, (YO, ssk) twice, YO, K1, K2tog, *ssk, K1, (YO, K2tog) twice, YO, K5, (YO, ssk) twice, YO, K1, K2tog, rep from* to last 10 sts, ssk, K1, (YO, K2tog) twice, YO, K3.

Row 15: K4, (YO, ssk) twice, YO, K2tog, *ssk, (YO, K2tog) twice, YO, K7, (YO, ssk) twice, YO, K2tog, rep from * to last 10 sts, ssk, (YO, K2tog) twice, YO, K4.

DRAGONFLY

Rows 17, 19, 21, 23, 25: K2tog, K3, (YO, ssk) twice, YO, K1, *K1, (YO, K2tog) twice, YO, K3, sl 2 kw-K1-p2sso, K3, (YO, ssk) twice, YO, K1, rep from * to last 10 sts, K1, (YO, K2tog) twice, YO, K3, ssk.

Row 27: K5, (YO, ssk) twice, K1, *K1, (K2tog, YO) twice, K9, (YO, ssk) twice, K1, rep from * to last 10 sts, K1, (K2tog, YO) twice, K5.

Row 29: K6, (YO, ssk) twice, *(K2tog, YO) twice, K11, (YO, ssk) twice, rep from * to last 10 sts, (K2tog, YO) twice, K6.

Row 31: K7, YO, ssk, K1, *K1, K2tog, YO, K13, YO, ssk, K1, rep from * to last 10 sts, K1, K2tog, YO, K7.

Row 33: K8, YO, ssk, *K2tog, YO, K15, YO, ssk, rep from * to last 10 sts, K2tog, YO, K8.

Row 34: Purl.

background

(58 sts)

Row 1: K8, YO, ssk, K2tog, YO, K34, YO, ssk, K2tog, YO, K8.

Row 2: Purl.

Rep rows 1 and 2 for patt.

dragonfly

(17-st panel)

Chart on page 25.

Row 1 (RS): K9, K2tog, YO, K6.

Row 2 and all WS rows: Purl.

Row 3: K8, K2tog, YO, K7.

Rows 5, 7, 9, and 11: K7, K2tog, YO, K8.

Row 13: YO, ssk, YO, ssk, K3, K2tog, YO, K4, K2tog, YO, K2tog, YO.

Row 15: K1, YO, ssk, YO, ssk, K2, K2tog, YO, K3, K2tog, YO, K2tog, YO, K1.

Row 17: K2, YO, ssk, YO, ssk, K1, K2tog, YO, K2, K2tog, YO, K2tog, YO, K2.

Row 19: K3, YO, ssk, YO, ssk, K2tog, YO, K1, K2tog, YO, K2tog, YO, K3.

Row 21: K3, K2tog, YO, K2tog, YO, K2tog, YO, K1, YO, ssk, YO, ssk, K3.

Row 23: K2, K2tog, YO, K2tog, YO, K1, K2tog, YO, K2, YO, ssk, YO, ssk, K2.

Row 25: K1, K2tog, YO, K2tog, YO, K2, K2tog, YO, K3, YO, ssk, YO, ssk, K1.

Row 27: K2tog, YO, K2tog, YO, K2, K2tog, YO, K1, YO, ssk, K2, YO, ssk, YO, ssk.

Row 29: K5, K2tog, YO, K2tog, YO, K1, YO, ssk, K5.

Row 31: K4, K2tog, YO, K2tog, YO, K1, YO, ssk, YO, ssk, K4.

Row 33: K5, K2tog, YO, K3, YO, ssk, K5.

Row 34: Purl.

WRAP (MAKE 2 PIECES)

CO 64 sts and knit 1 row. Setup row: Work 3 sts in edge-st patt, pm, work 58 sts in leaf patt to last 3 sts, pm, work 3 sts in edge-st patt. Complete a total of 34 rows in established patt, ending with row 34 of leaf patt.

Keeping first 3 and last 3 sts in edge-st patt, work background patt a total of 4 times (8 rows).

First dragonfly setup row: Work 3 sts in edge-st patt, K8, YO, ssk, K2tog, YO, K5, pm, work row 1 of dragonfly patt (17 sts), pm, K12, YO, ssk, K2tog, YO, K8, work 3 sts in edge-st patt. Cont in established patt, completing 34 rows of dragonfly patt.

Keeping first 3 and last 3 sts in edge-st patt, work background patt a total of 4 times (8 rows).

Second dragonfly setup row: Work 3 sts in edge-st patt, K8, YO, ssk, K2tog, YO, K12, pm, work row 1 of dragonfly patt (17 sts), pm, K5, YO, ssk, K2tog, YO, K8, work 3 sts in edge-st patt. Cont in established patt, completing 34 rows of dragonfly patt.

Keeping first 3 and last 3 sts in edge-st patt, work background patt a total of 4 times (8 rows).

Third dragonfly setup row: Work 3 sts in edge-st patt, K8, YO, ssk, K2tog, YO, K5, pm, work row 1 of dragonfly patt, pm, K12, YO, ssk, K2tog, YO, K8, work 3 sts in edge-st patt. Cont in established patt, completing 34 rows of dragonfly patt.

Keeping first 3 and last 3 sts in edge-st patt, work background patt until piece measures 30". Move all sts to st holder.

Rep for second piece, but do not move to st holder; leave on needles.

FINISHING

With right sides tog, work 3-needle BO (see page 74) to join pieces. Weave in all ends. Block using mist-and-pin method (see page 77).

SHERYL'S NOTES

Bonsai ribbon yarn, with its incredible drape and sheen, is made from renewable bamboo cellulose fibers. Bamboo is touted for its natural antibacterial qualities and UV protection.

Leaf

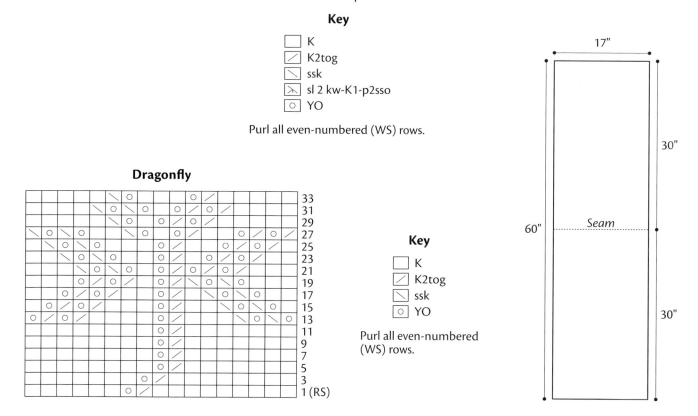

19-st rep

Key

☐	K
╱	K2tog
╲	ssk
⋏	sl 2 kw-K1-p2sso
○	YO

Purl all even-numbered (WS) rows.

Dragonfly

Key

☐	K
╱	K2tog
╲	ssk
○	YO

Purl all even-numbered (WS) rows.

FALL COLORS

Autumn is such a remarkable time, with spectacular fall colors traveling down a mountainside populated with deciduous trees such as maple, beech, oak, and hickory. The precise timing of the color change is hard to predict, but peak colors leave a lasting impression. This wrap, with a shoulder-hugging fit and "peak season" colors of hand-painted yarn, leaves a warm impression that will be treasured for years to come.

SKILL LEVEL

Easy ◼◼◻◻

FINISHED MEASUREMENTS

Top width: 33½"

Bottom width: 45½"

Length: 15"

MATERIALS

5 skeins of fingering weight from Claudia Hand Painted Yarns (100% merino wool; 50 g; 175 yds) in color John B **1**

Size 6 (4 mm) needles or size required to obtain gauge

Size 11 (8 mm) needles

Cable needle

Tapestry needle

GAUGE

20 sts = 4" in patt using size 6 and size 11 needles

STITCH PATTERN

fall colors

Row 1 (RS): With smaller needles, knit.

Rows 2, 3, and 4: With smaller needles, knit.

Row 5: With larger needles, knit.

Row 6: With larger needles, purl.

Rep rows 1–6 for patt.

WRAP

With smaller needles, CO 228 sts and knit 6 rows. With larger needles, knit 1 row, purl 1 row. With larger needles, K3, *sl 6 sts to cn, rotate cn 180° clockwise, K6 from cn, rep from * to last 3 sts, K3. With smaller needles, knit 1 row.

Work fall-colors patt a total of 6 times.

Dec 6 sts as follows: K8, (K2tog, K40) 5 times, K2tog, K8—222 sts. Beg with row 2, cont in fall-colors patt. Work patt a total of 11 times or until piece measures approximately 6", ending with row 6.

Dec 12 sts as follows: K8, (K2tog, K14) 11 times, K2tog, K8—182 sts. Beg with row 2, cont in fall-colors patt. Work patt a total of 19 times, ending with row 6.

Dec 14 sts as follows: K12, (K2tog, K10) 13 times, K2tog, K12—168 sts. Beg with row 2, cont in fall-colors patt, ending with row 6.

With larger needles, K3, *sl 6 sts to cn, rotate cn 180° clockwise, K6 from cn, rep from * to last 3 sts, K3. With smaller needles, knit 6 rows. BO (WS) all sts as follows: *P2tog, sl st on RH needle back to LH needle, rep from * until all sts are BO. Fasten off yarn.

TIES (WORK ON EACH SIDE)

With RS facing you and smaller needles, PU 59 sts along one short side. Knit 1 row.

Dec 11 sts as follows: K3, (K2tog, K3) 10 times, K2tog, K4—48 sts. Knit 1 row. Change to larger needles and work 8 rows in St st, decreasing first and last st EOR 4 times—40 sts. Cont in St st until tie measures 11". Change to smaller needles.

Dec 27 sts as follows: K4 tog, *K3tog, rep from * to end of row—13 sts. Cut yarn, leaving 12" tail. Thread tail through tapestry needle and draw yarn through rem sts, pulling tight. Fasten off end, leaving 12" tail. Use tail to seam side edges tog for about 2".

FINISHING

Weave in all ends. Block using mist method (see page 77).

Dec 8 sts as follows: K12, (K2tog, K26) 7 times, K2tog, K12—214 sts. Beg with row 2, cont in fall-colors patt. Work patt a total of 13 times.

Dec 10 sts as follows: K25, (K2tog, K16) 9 times, K2 tog, K25—204 sts. Beg with row 2, cont in fall-colors patt. Work patt a total of 15 times.

Dec 10 sts as follows: K20, (K2tog, K16) 9 times, K2tog, K20—194 sts. Beg with row 2, cont in fall-colors patt. Work patt a total of 17 times.

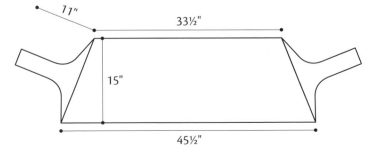

WATERFALL

Imagine a breathtaking cascade of water, tumbling over a rocky shelf, tucked between majestic mountains and filled with wildlife and rare wildflowers. This self-fringing wrap works up quickly, leaving plenty of time for daydreaming.

SKILL LEVEL

Intermediate ◖◼◼◻

FINISHED MEASUREMENTS

Width: 46"

Length without fringe: 17"

MATERIALS

2 skeins of Artesanal from AslanTrends (40% cotton, 30% alpaca, 30% polyamide; 100 g/3.5 oz; 218 yds) in color 218 🐑4️⃣

Size 9 (5.5 mm) needles or size required to obtain gauge

Size 11 (8 mm) needles

2 stitch markers

3 purchased metal clasps

GAUGE

12 sts = 4" in waterfall patt

STITCH PATTERN

waterfall

(Multiple of 6 + 14)

Chart on page 31.

K1B: Knit 1 from row below. Knit into center of st below next st on LH needle. Drop st above off LH needle.

Row 1 (RS): K1, K1B, K1, K1B, K1, P3, *K3, YO, P3, rep from * to last 6 sts, K6—inc 1 st per rep—7 sts total.

Row 2: K9, *P4, K3, rep from * to last 5 sts, K5.

Row 3: K1, K1B, K1, K1B, K1, P3, *K1, K2tog, YO, K1, P3, rep from * to last 6 sts, K6.

Row 4: K9, *P2, P2tog, K3, rep from * to last 5 sts, K5—dec 1 st per rep—7 sts total.

Row 5: K1, K1B, K1, K1B, K1, P3, *K1, YO, K2tog, P3, rep from * to last 6 sts, K6.

Row 6: K9, *P3, K3, rep from * to last 5 sts, K5.

Rep rows 1–6 for patt.

WATERFALL

WRAP

With smaller needles, CO 56 sts. Knit 2 rows. Work in waterfall patt until piece measures 42", ending with row 6.

Knit 2 rows. With larger needles, BO all sts loosely to last 6 sts. Leave these 6 sts on needle. Fasten off yarn. Sl 6 sts off needle and unravel down to CO edge to create fringe.

FINISHING

Make overhand knot near top of each fringe and slide knot up to knit edge before tightening. Make

a second overhand knot about half-way down fringe. Weave in all ends. Block using mist-and-pin method (see page 77). Mark placement of 3 metal clasps, approximately 2" apart. Sew metal hook along short edge of wrap. Sew metal eye to long edge.

SHERYL'S NOTES

For a sparkly look, after un-raveling the fringe, clip each loop and thread a large sequin onto each strand. Knot to secure in place.

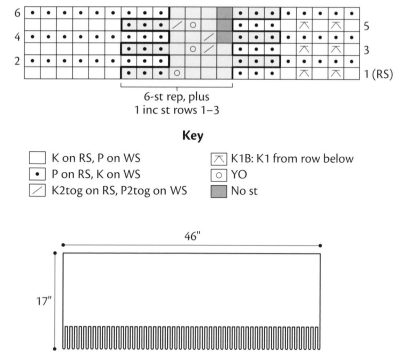

6-st rep, plus 1 inc st rows 1–3

Key

☐ K on RS, P on WS	⩓ K1B: K1 from row below
• P on RS, K on WS	○ YO
╱ K2tog on RS, P2tog on WS	▨ No st

46"

17"

FLAMES

Flames are the glowing, gaseous part of the phenomenon known as combustion. Dancing flames seem to have the capacity to mesmerize and hypnotize. With styling borrowed from a ruana, minimal seaming, and no shaping, this dancing flame-stitch wrap has similar ability to charm and captivate.

SKILL LEVEL

Intermediate ■■■☐

FINISHED MEASUREMENTS

Back: 46" x 17"

Front: 21" x 17"

MATERIALS

4 skeins of Jitterbug from Colinette Yarns, (100% merino; 110 g; 291 m) in color 71 Fire **1**

Size 8 (5 mm) needles or size required to obtain gauge

Tapestry needle

GAUGE

18 sts = 4" in patt

STITCH PATTERNS

seeded edge

(Multiple of 4 + 3)

Chart on page 35.

Row 1 (RS): P1, K1, *P3, K1, rep from *, P1.

Row 2 (WS): K3, *P1, K3, rep from *.

Rep rows 1 and 2 for patt.

flame

(Multiple of 7 + 4)

Chart on page 35.

Row 1 (RS): K3, *ssk, K5, YO, rep from *, K1.

Row 2 and all other WS rows: Purl.

Row 3: K3, *ssk, K4, YO, K1, rep from *, K1.

Row 5: K3, *ssk, K3, YO, K2, rep from *, K1.

Row 7: K3, *ssk, K2, YO, K3, rep from *, K1.

Row 9: K3, *ssk, K1, YO, K4, rep from *, K1.

Row 11: K3, *ssk, YO, K5, rep from *, K1.

Row 13: K1, *YO, K5, K2tog, rep from *, K3.

Row 15: K2, *YO, K4, K2tog, K1, rep from *, K2.

Row 17: K3, *YO, K3, K2tog, K2, rep from *, K1.

Row 19: K4, *YO, K2, K2tog, K3, rep from *.

FLAMES

Row 21: K5, *YO, K1, K2tog, K4, rep from *, *end last rep K3.*

Row 23: K6, *YO, K2tog, K5, rep from *, *end last rep K3.*

Row 24: Purl.

Rep rows 1–24 for patt.

BACK

CO 207 sts. Purl 1 row. Work 14 rows in seeded-edge patt, ending with WS row.

Setup row: Work 7 sts in established seeded-edge patt, pm, work row 1 of flame patt over 193 sts, pm, work

rem 7 sts in established seeded-edge patt. Cont in established patt, working 7 sts at each edge in seeded-edge patt and center 193 sts in flame patt for 4 total patt reps or until piece measures 16" when stretched slightly, ending with row 23 of flame patt.

Setup row: Work 7 sts in seeded-edge patt, remove marker, purl across row to marker, remove marker, work rem 7 sts in seeded-edge patt. Work 14 rows or for 2" in seeded-edge patt across all sts, ending with WS row. Purl 1 row. BO all sts loosely.

FRONT (MAKE 2)

CO 95 sts. Purl 1 row. Work 14 rows in seeded-edge patt, ending with WS row.

Setup row: Work 7 sts in established seeded-edge patt, pm, work row 1 of flame patt over 81 sts, pm, work rem 7 sts in established seeded-edge patt. Cont in established patt, working 7 sts at each edge in seeded-edge patt and center 81 sts in flame patt for 4 total patt reps or until piece measures 16" when stretched slightly, ending with row 23 of flame patt.

Setup row: Work 7 sts in seeded-edge patt, remove marker, purl across row to marker, remove marker, work rem 7 sts in seeded-edge patt. Work 14 rows or for 2" in seeded-edge patt

across all sts, ending with WS row.
Purl 1 row. BO all sts loosely.

FINISHING

Weave in all ends. Block to finished
measurements using mist-and-pin
method (see page 77). Sew front
to back, creating a shoulder seam
along bound-off edges (see page
75). Sew underarm seam along CO
edges of front and back, starting at
cuff and seaming for 6".

SHERYL'S NOTES

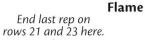

Make a much longer jacket
by working additional flame-
pattern repeats. You will need
to purchase more yarn.

Flame

*End last rep on
rows 21 and 23 here.*

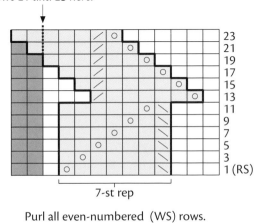

7-st rep

Purl all even-numbered (WS) rows.

Seeded Edge

4-st rep

Key

☐	K on RS, P on WS
•	P on RS, K on WS
╱	K2tog
╲	ssk
○	YO
▨	No st

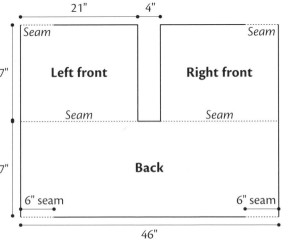

HEAVY RAIN

Rain is the condensation of atmospheric water vapor into drops heavy enough to fall. Here the sheets of heavy rain are depicted with drops, rounded at the bottom and narrow at the top. The cast-on edge has a picot of beads at the base of each drop. The mitered corner helps the wrap hug your shoulders. No need for a raincoat or umbrella with this rainstorm. Don't be put off by the length of the pattern; the wrap is easy to work.

SKILL LEVEL

Easy ◼◼☐☐

FINISHED MEASUREMENTS

Width at outside edge: 49"

Length: 15"

MATERIALS

6 skeins of Manos Silk Blend from Manos del Uruguay (30% silk, 70% merino extrafine wool; 50 g/1.75 oz; 150 yds) in color 3064 ◖3◗

Size 7 (4.5 mm) circular needle (24" or longer) or size required to obtain gauge

Size 8 (5 mm) circular needle (24" or longer)

1 stitch marker

222 clear beads, 4 mm

Big-eye beading needle

GAUGE

20 sts = 4" in patt

STITCH PATTERN

heavy rain with mitered corner

Chart for rep portion of patt on page 40.

Row 1 (RS): K2, *P4, YO, P2tog, rep from * to 17 sts before marker, P15, P2tog tbl, sl marker, P2tog, P11, *P4, YO, P2tog, rep from * to last 6 sts, P4, K2.

Row 2: Knit to 2 sts before marker, K2tog, sl marker, ssk, knit to end.

Row 3: K2, *P4, K1, P1, rep from * to 15 sts before marker, P13, P2tog tbl, sl marker, P2tog, P9, *P4, K1, P1, rep from * to last 6 sts, P4, K2.

Row 4: K2, knit the knit sts and purl the purl sts as they face you to marker, sl marker, knit the knit sts and purl the purl sts to last 2 sts, K2.

Row 5: K2, *P4, K1, P1, rep from * to 14 sts before marker, P12, P2tog tbl, sl marker, P2tog, P8, *P4, K1, P1, rep from * to last 6 sts, P4, K2.

Row 6: K2, knit the knit sts and purl the purl sts as they face you to 2 sts before marker, K2tog, sl marker, ssk, knit the knit sts and purl the purl sts to last 2 sts, K2.

Row 7: K2, *P1, YO, P2tog, P3, rep from * to 12 sts before marker, P1, YO, P2tog, P7, P2tog tbl, sl marker, P2tog, P6, *P1, YO, P2tog, P3, rep from * to last 6 sts, P1, YO, P2tog, P1, K2.

Row 8: Knit.

Row 9: K2, *P1, K1, P4, rep from * to 11 sts before marker, P1, K1, P7, P2tog tbl, sl marker, P2tog, P5, *P1, K1, P4, rep from * to last 6 sts, P1, K1, P2, K2.

Row 10: K2, knit the knit sts and purl the purl sts as they face you to 2 sts before marker, K2tog, sl marker, ssk, knit the knit sts and purl the purl sts to last 2 sts, K2.

Row 11: K2, *P1, K1, P4, rep from* to 9 sts before marker, P1, K1, P5, P2tog tbl, sl marker, P2tog, P3, *P1, K1, P4, rep from * to last 6 sts, P1, K1, P2, K2.

Row 12: K2, knit the knit sts and purl the purl sts as they face you to marker, sl marker, knit the knit sts and purl the purl sts to last 2 sts, K2.

Row 13: K2, *P4, YO, P2tog, rep from * to 20 sts before marker, P18, P2tog tbl, sl marker, P2tog, P14, *P4, YO, P2tog, rep from * to last 6 sts, P4, K2.

Row 14: Knit to 2 sts before marker, K2tog, sl marker, ssk, knit to end.

Row 15: K2, *P4, K1, P1, rep from* to 18 sts before marker, P16, P2tog tbl, sl marker, P2tog, P12, *P4, K1, P1, rep from * to last 6 sts, P4, K2.

Row 16: K2, knit the knit sts and purl the purl sts as they face you to marker, sl marker, knit the knit sts and purl the purl sts to last 2 sts, K2.

Row 17: K2 *P4, K1, P1, rep from * to 17 sts before marker, P15, P2tog tbl, sl marker, P2tog, P11, *P4, K1, P1, rep from * to last 6 sts, P4, K2.

Row 18: K2, knit the knit sts and purl the purl sts as they face you to 2 sts before marker, K2tog, sl marker, ssk, knit the knit sts and purl the purl sts to last 2 sts, K2.

Row 19: K2, *P1, YO, P2tog, P3, rep from * to 15 sts before marker, P1, YO, P2tog, P10, P2tog tbl, sl marker, P2tog, P9, *P1, YO, P2tog, P3, rep from * to last 6 sts, P1, YO, P2tog, P1, K2.

Row 20: Knit.

Row 21: K2, *P1, K1, P4, rep from * to 14 sts before marker, P1, K1, P10, P2tog tbl, sl marker, P2tog, P8, *P1, K1, P4, rep from * to last 6 sts, P1, K1, P2, K2.

Row 22: K2, knit the knit sts and purl the purl sts as they face you to 2 sts before marker, K2tog, sl marker, ssk, knit the knit sts and purl the purl sts to last 2 sts, K2.

Row 23: K2, *P1, K1, P4, rep from* to 12 sts before marker, P1, K1, P8, P2tog tbl, sl marker, P2tog, P6, *P1, K1, P4, rep from * to last 6 sts, P1, K1, P2, K2.

Row 24: K2, knit the knit sts and purl the purl sts as they face you to 2 sts before marker, K2tog, sl marker, ssk, knit the knit sts and purl the purl sts to last 2 sts, K2.

Row 25: K2, *P4, YO, P2tog, rep from * to 23 sts before marker, P21, P2tog tbl, sl marker, P2tog, P17, *P4, YO, P2tog, rep from * to last 6 sts, P4, K2.

Row 26: Knit to 2 sts before marker, K2tog, sl marker, ssk, knit to end.

Row 27: K2, *P4, K1, P1, rep from* to 21 sts before marker, P19, P2tog tbl, sl marker, P2tog, P15, *P4, K1, P1, rep from * to last 6 sts, P4, K2.

Row 28: K2, knit the knit sts and purl the purl sts as they face you to marker, sl marker, knit the knit sts and purl the purl sts to last 2 sts, K2.

Row 29: K2, *P4, K1, P1, rep from* to 20 sts before marker, P18, P2tog tbl, sl marker, P2tog, P14, *P4, K1, P1, rep from * to last 6 sts, P4, K2.

Row 30: K2, knit the knit sts and purl the purl sts as they face you to 2 sts before marker, K2tog, sl marker, ssk, knit the knit sts and purl the purl sts to last 2 sts, K2.

Row 31: K2, *P1, YO, P2tog, P3, rep from * to 18 sts before marker, P1, YO, P2tog, P13, P2tog tbl, sl marker, P2tog, P12, *P1, YO, P2tog, P3, rep from * to last 6 sts, P1, YO, P2tog, P1, K2.

Row 32: Knit.

Row 33: K2, *P1, K1, P4, rep from * to 17 sts before marker, P1, K1, P13, P2tog tbl, sl marker, P2tog, P11, *P1, K1, P4, rep from * to last 6 sts, P1, K1, P2, K2.

Row 34: K2, knit the knit sts and purl the purl sts as they face you to 2 sts before marker, K2tog, sl marker, ssk, knit the knit sts and purl the purl sts to last 2 sts, K2.

Row 35: K2, *P1, K1, P4, rep from * to 15 sts before marker, P1, K1, P11, P2tog tbl, sl marker, P2tog, P9, *P1, K1, P4, rep from * to last 6 sts, P1, K1, P2, K2.

Row 36: K2, knit the knit sts and purl the purl sts as they face you to marker, sl maker, knit the knit sts and purl the purl sts to last 2 sts, K2.

Row 37: K2, *P4, YO, P2tog, rep from * to 26 sts before marker, P24, P2tog tbl, sl marker, P2tog, P20, *P4, YO, P2tog, rep from * to last 6 sts, P4, K2.

Row 38: Knit to 2 sts before marker, K2tog, sl marker, ssk, knit to end.

Row 39: K2, *P4, K1, P1, rep from * to 24 sts before marker, P22, P2tog tbl, sl marker, P2tog, P18, *P4, K1, P1, rep from * to last 6 sts, P4, K2.

Row 40: K2, knit the knit sts and purl the purl sts as they face you to marker, sl marker, knit the knit sts and purl the purl sts to last 2 sts, K2.

Row 41: K2, *P4, K1, P1, rep from* to 23 sts before marker, P21, P2tog tbl, sl marker, P2tog, P17, *P4, K1, P1, rep from * to last 6 sts, P4, K2.

Row 42: K2, knit the knit sts and purl the purl sts as they face you to 2 sts before marker, K2tog, sl marker, ssk, knit the knit sts and purl the purl sts to last 2 sts, K2.

Row 43: K2, *P1, YO, P2tog, P3, rep from * to 21 sts before marker, P1, YO, P2tog, P16, P2tog tbl, sl marker, P2tog, P15, *P1, YO, P2tog, P3, rep from * to last 6 sts, P1, YO, P2tog, P1, K2.

Row 44: Knit.

Row 45: K2, *P1, K1, P4, rep from * to 20 sts before marker, P1, K1, P16, P2tog tbl, sl marker, P2tog, P14, *P1, K1, P4, rep from * to last 6 sts, P1, K1, P2, K2.

Row 46: K2, knit the knit sts and purl the purl sts as they face you to 2 sts before marker, K2tog, sl marker, ssk, knit the knit sts and purl the purl sts to last 2 sts, K2.

Row 47: K2, *P1, K1, P4, rep from * to 18 sts before marker, P1, K1, P14, P2tog tbl, sl marker, P2tog, P12, *P1, K1, P4, rep from * to last 6 sts, P1, K1, P2, K2.

Row 48: K2, knit the knit sts and purl the purl sts as they face you to marker, sl marker, knit the knit sts and purl the purl sts to last 2 sts, K2.

Rep rows 1–48 for patt.

WRAP

3B (place 3 beads): Sl 3 beads up next to needle; do not pull beads through when making next CO st. Beads will hang on back of work while working CO row.

Using big-eye needle, string 222 beads onto yarn. Using larger needle, cable CO 482 sts as follows: CO 7, 3B, CO 1, (CO 5, 3B, CO 1) 36 times, CO 17, pm, CO 18, 3B, CO 1 (CO 5, 3B, CO 1) 36 times, CO 6. Do not join; wrap is knit back and forth (circular needle is used to accommodate large number of sts). Change to smaller needle and purl 1 row. Beg heavy rain with mitered corner patt and work 96 rows. Knit 4 rows. Using larger needle, BO all sts loosely.

FINISHING

Weave in all ends. Block using mist method (see page 77).

SHERYL'S NOTES

If desired, you could make the wrap without the beads. Simply cast on and work as directed.

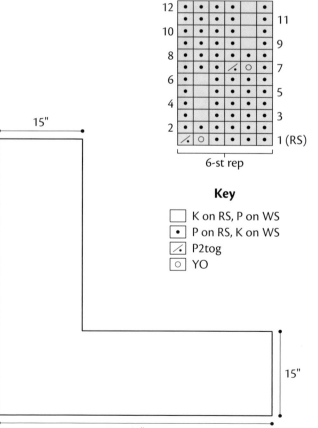

6-st rep

Key

☐	K on RS, P on WS
•	P on RS, K on WS
⟋	P2tog
○	YO

15"

49"

49"

15"

MILKY WAY

Best seen in the country away from city lights, the Milky Way appears as a hazy luminous band of light that stretches across the night sky. The cosmic clusters of knitted stars bordered by rickrack ribbing, and the soft and supple silk yarn create a wrap that you'll want to wear day and night.

SKILL LEVEL
Easy ◼◼◻◻

FINISHED MEASUREMENTS
Width: 68"

Length: 15"

MATERIALS
5 skeins of Pure Silk DK from Rowan Classic Yarns (100% silk; 50 g; 137 yds) in color SH156 Tranquil **3**

Size 9 (5.5 mm) needles or size required to obtain gauge

Size 11 (8 mm) needles

2 stitch markers

GAUGE
17 sts = 4" in star pattern

STITCH PATTERNS

rickrack ribbing
(Multiple of 3 + 1)

T2K (Twist 2 Knit): Wyib, take RH needle behind left, skip first st on LH needle, knit into back loop of second st and leave on needle; knit skipped st through front loop and sl both sts off LH needle.

T2P (Twist 2 Purl): Wyif, skip first st on LH needle, purl second st and leave on needle; purl skipped st and sl both sts off LH needle.

Row 1 (RS): P1, *T2K, P1, rep from *.

Row 2: K1, *T2P, K1, rep from*.

Rep rows 1 and 2 for patt.

star
(Multiple of 3)

Row 1 (RS): K2, *YO, K3, pass first st of K3 sts over second and third sts, rep from * to last st, K1.

Row 2: Purl.

Row 3: K1, *K3, pass first st of K3 sts over second and third sts, YO, rep from * to last 2 sts, K2.

Row 4: Purl.

Rep rows 1–4 for patt.

42

WRAP

With smaller needles, CO 64 sts and knit 1 row. Work 7 rows in rickrack-ribbing patt, ending with row 1.

Inc row: Work 10 sts in rickrack-ribbing patt, pm, M1, purl to last 10 sts, pm, work rem sts in rickrack-ribbing patt—65 sts.

Setup row: Work 10 sts in rickrack-ribbing patt, sl marker, work 45 sts in star patt, sl marker, work 10 sts in rickrack-ribbing patt. Cont in patt established in setup row until piece measures about 67", ending with row 3 of star patt.

Dec row: Work 10 sts in rickrack-ribbing patt, remove marker, P2tog, purl to marker, remove marker, work to end in rickrack-ribbing patt.

Cont in rickrack-ribbing patt for 7 rows. With larger needle, BO all sts loosely in K1, P2 ribbing.

FINISHING

Weave in all ends. Block using mist method (see page 77).

SHERYL'S NOTES

Take full advantage of the incredible drape of the silk yarn and wear either as a scarf around your neck or over your shoulders as a shawl.

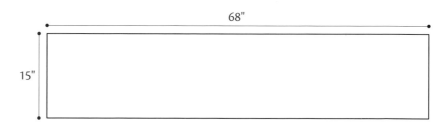

ORCHIDS

For centuries, orchids have been associated with mystery and romance. Enjoy the elegance and fascination of these exotic blooms without having to water, feed, or adjust the light. Brighten your wardrobe with this beautiful V-shaped, garter-stitch wrap with its center-back panel of blooming orchids and a delicate, airy yarn-over edge.

SKILL LEVEL

Intermediate ◼◼◼▢

FINISHED MEASUREMENTS

Width at widest point: 35"

Center back length: 24"

Front length: 25"

MATERIALS

3 skeins of Superior from Filatura Di Crosa (70% cashmere, 30% silk; 25 g/.88 oz; 328 yds) in color 22 Orchid [2]

Size 6 (4 mm) needles or size required to obtain gauge

2 stitch markers

1 ring, 1" diameter (optional)

GAUGE

22 sts = 4" in garter st

STITCH PATTERNS

garter increase

All rows: YO, knit to end of row.

Rep for patt.

orchid panel

(19-st panel)

Chart on page 47.

Row 1 (RS): K2, YO, K4, K2tog, YO, sl 2 kw-K1-p2sso, YO, ssk, K4, YO, K2.

Row 2 and all WS rows: Purl.

Row 3: K3, YO, K2, K3tog, YO, K3, YO, sl 1 K2tog-psso, K2, YO, K3.

Row 5: K4, YO, K1, K2tog, YO, K1, sl 2 kw-K1-p2sso, K1, YO, ssk, K1, YO, K4.

Row 7: K5, YO, K2tog, YO, K1, sl 2 kw-K1-p2sso, K1, YO, ssk, YO, K5.

Row 9: K3, K2tog, YO, K1, YO, K2, sl 2 kw-K1-p2sso, K2, YO, K1, YO, ssk, K3.

Row 11: K2, K2tog, YO, K3, YO, K1, sl 2 kw-K1-p2sso, K1, YO, K3, YO, ssk, K2.

Row 13: K1, K2tog, YO, K5, YO, sl 2 kw-K1-p2sso, YO, K5, YO, ssk, K1.

Row 14: Purl.

Rep rows 1–14 for panel.

ORCHIDS

garter decrease

Work both front sides at same time.

All rows: YO, K2tog, knit to inner edge. On second front side and with second ball of yarn, YO, K3tog, knit to end.

Rep for patt.

YARN OVER AT THE BEGINNING OF A ROW

Hold yarn to the front of your work and insert right-hand needle into the first stitch as if to knit. Bring yarn over the right-hand needle to the back and knit the first stitch. You will have two loops on your right-hand needle.

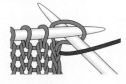

WRAP

CO 15 sts. Work in garter-inc patt until 21 sts on needle.

Setup row: YO, K1, pm, work row 1 of orchid panel over 19 sts, pm, K1.

Cont in garter-inc patt to marker, work 19-st orchid panel to marker, and work garter-inc patt to end of row. Work in established patt until 189 sts are on needle (85 sts on each side of markers), ending with row 14 of orchid panel.

Work 4 rows of garter-inc patt, leave markers in place but work garter st instead of orchid panel sts—193 sts.

Divide for front as follows: YO, knit to marker, sl marker, K9, BO 1 (center st), cont knitting across row. Working both sides of front at same time and using 2 balls of yarn (1 ball for each side), beg garter-dec patt, removing markers. Cont working both fronts in garter-dec patt, decreasing 1 st each row, until 3 sts rem. K3tog. Fasten off yarn.

FINISHING

Weave in all ends. Block using mist method (see page 77).

SHERYL'S NOTES

To make smaller, triangular-shaped shawl, work patt until 193 sts on needle, then BO all sts very loosely. You will need only 2 skeins of yarn. Wear with ends tied in front with half knot and slide ring up to knot.

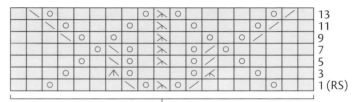

13
11
9
7
5
3
1 (RS)

19-st panel

Key

- ☐ K
- ╱ K2tog
- ╲ ssk
- ⋀ sl 1-K2tog-psso
- ⋋ sl 2 kw-K1-p2sso
- ⋀ K3tog
- ◌ YO

Purl all even-numbered (WS) rows.

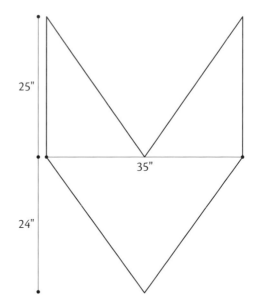

25"

24"

35"

RASPBERRIES

Raspberries found at roadside farm stands are always lush and bursting with juice. Better yet, pick your own. This top-down cape allows you to enjoy the bumpy texture of raspberries when they are out of season—and always without thorns and stains.

SKILL LEVEL

Intermediate ◼◼◼▢

FINISHED MEASUREMENTS

Small/Medium (Large/Extra Large)

Bottom circumference: 64¾ (73¾)"

Length: 22"

MATERIALS

10 (11) skeins of Donegal Luxury Tweed from Debbie Bliss (85% wool, 15% angora; 50 g; 85 m) in color 360017 **4**

Size 8 (5 mm) circular needle (29" or longer) or size required to obtain gauge

Size 7 (4.5 mm) circular needle

Size 10 (6 mm) needles

4 stitch markers

1 button, 1¼" diameter

GAUGE

16 sts = 4" in St st

STITCH PATTERNS

increase a

Row 1: *Knit to 1 st before marker, K1f&b, sl marker, K1f&b, rep from *, knit to end.

Row 2: Purl.

Rep rows 1 and 2 for patt.

increase b

Row 1: Knit.

Row 2: Purl.

Row 3: *Knit to 1 st before marker, K1f&b, sl marker, K1f&b, rep from *, knit to end.

Row 4: Purl.

Rep rows 1–4 for patt.

raspberries

(Multiple of 4 + 3)

Row 1 (RS): K1, (K1, K1tbl, K1) in next st, *P3, (K1, K1tbl, K1) in next st, rep from * to last st, end K1.

Row 2: K4, P3tog, *K3, P3tog, rep from* to last 4 sts, end K4.

Row 3: K1, P3, *(K1, K1tbl, K1) in next st, P3, rep from * to last st, end K1.

Row 4: K1, P3tog, *K3, P3tog, rep from * to last st, end K1.

Rep rows 1–4 for patt.

RASPBERRIES

WRAP

Wrap is knit from top down. With size 8 circular needle, CO 48 (54) sts. Do not join; piece is knit back and forth (circular needle is to accommodate large number of sts).

Purl 1 row.

Setup row: K1, pm, K11, pm, K24 (30), pm, K11, pm, K1. Purl 1 row.

Work inc-A patt 7 times, ending with row 2—104 (110) sts. Using backward-loop method (see page 74), CO 9 (11) sts, work across row in inc-A patt. CO 9 (11) sts and purl across row—130 (140) sts. Cont working in inc-A patt 14 (17) times—242 (276) sts.

Work inc-B patt 2 times—258 (292) sts. Work in St st (knit 1 row, purl 1 row) until piece measures 17" from back of center neck, ending with purl row. Knit 1 row. Knit 1 row, inc 1 (3) sts evenly across row—259 (295) sts.

Work in raspberries patt until piece measures 22", ending with row 4. Knit 2 rows. Using size 10 needles, BO all sts loosely.

SHERYL'S NOTES

Omit the buttonhole and close the front with a shawl stickpin or purchased metal hook and eye.

FINISHING

right front band

With RS facing you and size 8 needle, PU 87 sts along right front. Knit 1 row. Work 8 rows in raspberries patt. Work buttonhole as follows: Knit to 6 sts before end of row, BO 3 sts, knit last 2 sts. Turn work. Knit 3 sts, CO 3 sts, cont knitting across row. Using size 10 needles, BO all sts loosely.

left front band

With RS facing you and size 8 needle, PU 87 sts along left front. Knit 1 row. Work 8 rows in raspberries patt. Knit 2 rows. Using size 10 needles, BO all sts loosely.

collar

With size 7 needle, beg at top center of right front band, PU 87 (95) sts evenly around neck, ending at center of left front band. Work 4 rows in K1, P1 ribbing. Knit 1 row. Change to size 8 needle and knit 1 row. Beg raspberries patt; RS of raspberries patt will be on the inside (WS) of wrap until collar is turned out. Cont in raspberries patt until collar measures 4" above ribbing, ending with row 4. Knit 2 rows. BO all sts loosely.

Weave in all ends. Block using mist method (see page 77). Position button and sew in place.

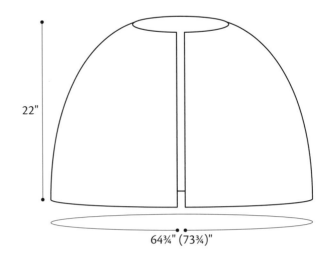

22"

64¾" (73¾)"

ROSES

An ancient symbol of love and beauty, the rose was sacred to many goddesses, including Isis, the Egyptian goddess of nature, and Aphrodite, the Greek goddess of love. Drape yourself with this uniquely shaped wrap—its distinctive embossed rose is framed by a double moss pattern—and feel like a goddess. Wear it with the square in back and the long ends in front.

SKILL LEVEL

Easy ◀■□□

FINISHED MEASUREMENTS

Back panel: 12" x 12"

Front panel: 12" x 30"

MATERIALS

6 skeins of Karma from S. Charles (63% wool, 27% angora, 10% nylon; 50 g/1.75 oz; 119 yds) in color 07 **5**

Size 10½ (6.5 mm) needles or size required to obtain gauge

2 stitch markers

Tapestry needle

GAUGE

14 sts and 18 rows = 4" in St st

STITCH PATTERN

double moss

(Multiple of 2)

Row 1: *K1, P1 rep from *.

Row 2: Knit the knit sts and purl the purl sts as they face you.

Row 3: *P1, K1, rep from *.

Row 4: Knit the knit sts and purl the purl sts as they face you.

Rep rows 1–4 for patt.

WRAP

Chart for rose patt is on page 53.

back

CO 48 sts and work in double moss patt for 6 rows. Work next 6 rows as follows: cont in double moss patt for 6 sts, work in St st to last 6 sts, cont in double moss patt.

Set up rose-patt row: Cont in double moss patt for 6 sts, work 4 sts in St st, pm, work row 1 of rose patt (from chart) over 29 sts, pm, work in St st for 3 sts, cont in double moss patt for 6 sts. Cont in established patt for 37 rows.

Work 3 rows as follows: cont in double moss patt for 6 sts, work in St st, beg with purl row to last 6 sts, removing markers as you come to them, cont in double moss patt. Work 6 rows in double moss patt. BO all sts loosely.

ROSES

front (make 2)

CO 48 sts. Work in double moss patt for 6 rows. Work next 6 rows as follows: cont in double moss patt for 6 sts, work in St st to last 6 sts, cont in double moss patt.

Set up rose-patt row: Cont in double moss patt for 6 sts, work 4 sts in St st, pm, work row 1 of rose chart over 29 sts, pm, work in St st for 3 sts, cont in double moss patt for 6 sts. Cont in established patt for 37 rows.

Work rem front as follows: cont in double moss patt for 6 sts, work in St st, beg with purl row to last 6 sts, removing markers as you come to them, cont in double moss patt. Work in established patt until piece measures 30". BO all sts loosely. Rep for second piece.

FINISHING

Sew bound-off edge of fronts to back; see schematic for placement. Weave in all ends. Block using mist-and-pin method (see page 77).

SHERYL'S NOTES

To help keep your place while working the graph, place a sticky note on the row above the row you are working. This allows you to see the pattern you are building on.

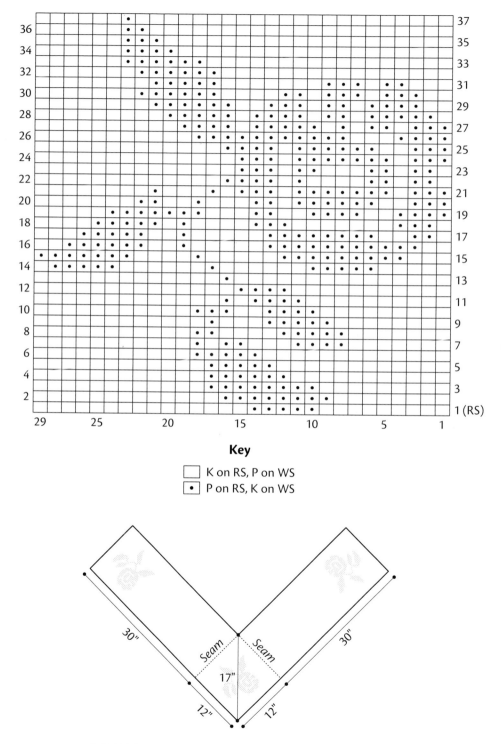

Key

☐	K on RS, P on WS
⊡	P on RS, K on WS

SANDY BEACH

Walk barefoot along a beach and experience the pleasant feeling of warm sand between your toes and on the soles of your feet. Wear this little showcase wrap around your neck and feel the pebbly texture of this reversible stitch pattern along with the warmth of the delectably smooth, silky fibers.

SKILL LEVEL

Beginner ■□□□

FINISHED MEASUREMENTS

Width: 46"

Length: 9"

MATERIALS

1 skein of Mooi from Louet (70% bamboo, 15% bison, 15% cashmere; 50 g; 350 yds) in color Natural

Size 4 (3.5 mm) needles or size required to obtain gauge

Size 8 (5 mm) needles

1 faux shell 1⅝" diameter ring (optional)

GAUGE

29 sts = 4" in sandy-beach patt

STITCH PATTERN

sandy beach

(Multiple of 2 + 1)

Row 1 (RS): Knit.

Row 2: K1, *P1, K1, rep from *.

Rep rows 1 and 2 for patt.

WRAP

With smaller needles, CO 67 sts. Knit 1 row. Work in sandy-beach patt until piece measures about 44", ending with row 2. Knit 2 rows. Using larger needles, BO all sts loosely.

FINISHING

Weave in ends. Block using wet method (see page 77). Sew faux-shell ring in the middle of one short end.

SHERYL'S NOTES

Metal, wood, and bamboo needles may be too slick for the Mooi yarn. For better yarn control, try plastic needles. Bryspun needles, known for their nice points, were used for this piece.

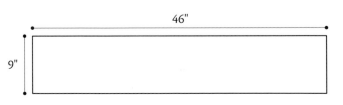

46"

9"

SANDY BEACH

SNOWDRIFT

Deposits of blown snow create undulating patterns and impressive drifts that cast eerie shadows over the icy landscape. Snuggle in this wrap with its center snowdrift cable and shadow ribbing, and forget about the blowing snow.

SKILL LEVEL

Intermediate ■■■□

FINISHED MEASUREMENTS

Width: 76"

Length: 25"

MATERIALS

10 skeins of Green Mountain Green from Green Mountain Spinnery (60% fine wool, 40% kid mohair; 2 oz; 120 yds) in color 3189 **5**

Size 10½ (6.5 mm) needles or size required to obtain gauge

Cable needle

4 stitch markers

3 buttons, 1½" diameter

GAUGE

14 sts = 4" in shadow ribbing patt

STITCH PATTERNS

shadow ribbing

(Multiple of 3 + 2)

Row 1 (RS): Purl.

Row 2: K2, *(P1, K2), rep from *.

Rep rows 1 and 2 for patt.

snowdrift cable

(24-st panel)

Chart on page 58.

6/6CF: Sl 6 sts to cn and hold in front, K6, K6 from cn.

6/6CB: Sl 6 sts to cn and hold in back, K6, K6 from cn.

Rows 1, 3, and 5 (RS): Knit.

Row 2 and all WS rows: Purl.

Row 7: K6, 6/6CF, K6.

Rows 9, 11, 13, and 15: Knit.

Row 17: 6/6CF, 6/6CB.

Row 19: Knit.

Row 20: Purl.

Rep rows 1–20 for patt.

WRAP

CO 92 sts. Work 11 rows in shadow-ribbing patt.

Setup row: Cont in shadow-ribbing patt for 35 sts, pm, P1, pm, P1, (P1f&b, P4) 3 times, P1f&b, P3, pm, P1, pm, cont in shadow-ribbing patt 35 sts to end of row—96 sts. Establish patt as follows: work 35 sts in shadow-ribbing patt, sl marker,

work 1 St st, sl marker, work 24 sts in snowdrift-cable patt, sl marker, work 1 St st, work 35 sts in shadow-ribbing patt. Work in established patt until piece measures 12", ending with WS row.

Shape buttonhole as follows:

Row 1 (RS): Work 4 sts in established patt. BO 3 sts, cont across row in established patt.

Row 2: Work across row in established patt to buttonhole, CO 3 sts over bound-off gap, work last 4 sts in patt.

Work 14 rows in established patt. Work buttonhole over 2 rows. Rep 1 more time for a total of 3 buttonholes. Cont in established patt until piece measures 73", ending with row 15 of snowdrift cable patt.

Work dec row as follows: cont in shadow-ribbing patt for 35 sts, P1, P1, (P2tog, P4) 3 times, P2tog, P3, P1, work 35 sts in shadow-ribbing patt, removing markers as you come to them—92 sts.

Work 11 rows in shadow-ribbing patt. BO all sts as follows: K2tog, *place st just worked back on LH needle and K2tog (st just worked and new st), rep from * until only 1 loop on RH needle rem. Fasten off yarn.

FINISHING

Weave in all ends. Mark button placement and sew in place. Block using mist-and-pin method (see page 77).

SHERYL'S NOTES

Green Mountain Spinnery was producing environmentally green yarn before green was even in. The Green Mountain Green fibers are greenspun with vegetable-based soaps and oils to preserve the natural sheen and resilience of the yarn.

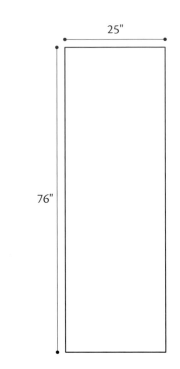

25"

76"

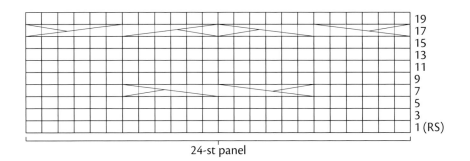

19
17
15
13
11
9
7
5
3
1 (RS)

24-st panel

Key

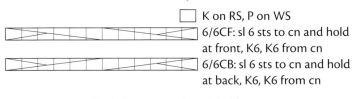

K on RS, P on WS

6/6CF: sl 6 sts to cn and hold at front, K6, K6 from cn

6/6CB: sl 6 sts to cn and hold at back, K6, K6 from cn

Purl all even-numbered (WS) rows.

SNOWFLAKES

Snowflakes, precipitation in the form of small white ice crystals directly formed from the water vapor in air that's below freezing temperature, are amazing. The impressive snowflakes on this triangle shawl, tipped with a crocheted triple picot edge, will lie on your shoulders, but unlike real snow, these flakes will not turn slushy or melt.

SKILL LEVEL

Intermediate ■■■□

FINISHED MEASUREMENTS

Top width without crocheted edge: 59"

Longest length without crocheted edge: 33"

MATERIALS

8 skeins of Palace from Berroco (50% merino wool, 50% silk; 50 g/1.75 oz; 103 yds) in color 8901 ④

Size 9 (5.5 mm) needles or size required to obtain gauge

Size G (4 mm) crochet hook

GAUGE

15 sts = 4" in St st

STITCH PATTERNS

M1R: M1 increase with right slant: On knit side, insert left needle from back to front under horizontal ladder. Knit this lifted strand through front to twist st to right.

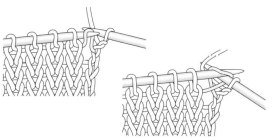

M1L: M1 increase with left slant: On knit side, insert left needle from front to back under horizontal ladder. Knit this lifted strand through back to twist st to left.

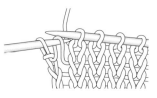

increase

Row 1 (RS): K1, M1R, knit to last 2 sts, M1L, K1.

Row 2: Purl.

Rep rows 1 and 2 for patt.

SNOWFLAKES

snowflake

(Multiple of 8 + edge + inc)

Chart at right.

Row 1 (RS): K1, M1R, knit to last st, M1L, K1.

Row 2 and all WS rows: Purl.

Row 3: K1, M1R, K5, *ssk, YO, K1, YO, K2tog, K3, rep from * to last 3 sts, K2, M1L, K1.

Row 5: K1, M1R, K7, *YO, sl 2 kw-K1-p2sso, YO, K5, rep from * to last 3 sts, K2, M1L, K1.

Row 7: K1, M1R, K7, *ssk, YO, K1, YO, K2tog, K3, rep from * to last 5 sts, K4, M1L, K1.

Row 8: Purl.

Rep rows 1–8 for patt.

WRAP

CO 9 sts and purl 1 row. Work in inc patt until 15 sts are on needle, ending with row 2. Beg snowflake patt. One snowflake is added for each 8-row patt rep. Cont until patt rep with 25 snowflakes is completed—215 sts. Work 8 rows in inc patt, ending with WS row—223 sts. BO sts loosely.

FINISHING

Weave in all ends. With crochet hook and RS facing, sc along entire edge, working 2 sc in each corner st. Join with sl st. Work triple picot as follows: *work 6 sc, (ch 3, sl st in third st from hook) 3 times, rep from *. Join with sl st and fasten off yarn.

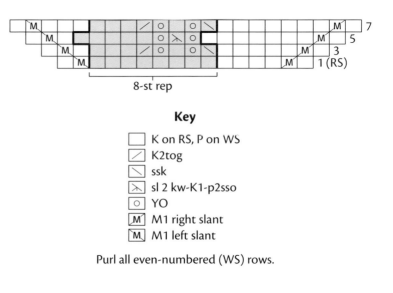

8-st rep

Key

☐	K on RS, P on WS
╱	K2tog
╲	ssk
⋏	sl 2 kw-K1-p2sso
○	YO
M	M1 right slant
M	M1 left slant

Purl all even-numbered (WS) rows.

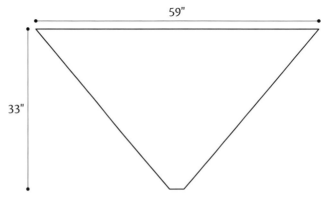

59"

33"

SUNSET

The setting sun, streaking the sky with vibrant shades of red and orange amid hints of purple, can be breathtaking, however fleeting. This top-down swirled poncho, trimmed in diagonal ribbing, will be a favorite for years.

SKILL LEVEL

Easy ◖■□□

FINISHED MEASUREMENTS

Neck circumference: 25"

Bottom circumference: 120"

Length: 17"

MATERIALS

5 skeins of Lion and Lamb from Lorna's Laces (50% silk, 50% wool; 205 yds) in color 620 Bittersweet (4)

Size 7 (4.5 mm) circular needle (24") or size required to obtain gauge

Size 8 (5 mm) circular needle (24") or size required to obtain gauge

Size 9 (5.5 mm) circular needle (60")

Size 10 (6 mm) needles

1 stitch marker

GAUGE

18 sts = 4" in St st on size 8 needle

16 sts = 4" in St st on size 9 needle

STITCH PATTERNS

sunset spiral

(8 sections)

Rnd 1: *K14, YO, rep from * to end of rnd—inc 8 sts.

Rnd 2 and all even number rnds: Knit.

Rnd 3: *K15, YO, rep from * to end of rnd—inc 8 sts.

Rnd 5: *K16, YO, rep from * to end of rnd—inc 8 sts.

Rnd 7: *K17, YO, rep from * to end of rnd—inc 8 sts.

Rnd 9: *K18, YO, rep from * to end of rnd—inc 8 sts.

Rnd 11: *K19, YO, rep from * to end of rnd—inc 8 sts.

Rnd 13: *K20, YO, rep from * to end of rnd—inc 8 sts.

Rnd 14: Knit.

Work in established patt, inc 8 sts every other rnd, moving YO 1 st.

swirl-ribbing border

(Multiple of 6)

Rnd 1: *K3, P3, rep from *.

Rnd 2: P1, *K3, P3, rep from * to last 5 sts, K3, P2.

Rnd 3: P2, *K3, P3, rep from * to last 4 sts, K3, P1.

Rnd 4: *P3, K3, rep from *.

Rnd 5: K1, *P3, K3, rep from * to last 5 sts, P3, K2.

Rnd 6: K2, *P3, K3, rep from * to last 4 sts, P3, K1.

Rep rnds 1–6 for patt.

WRAP

Using size 8 circular needle, CO 112 sts, join in rnd, and pm. Knit 2 rnds. Work in sunset-spiral patt. After rnd 14, cont to work in established patt, inc 8 sts in 1 rnd, followed by a knit rnd without incs. To maintain spiral, work YO 1 st farther from beg on each inc rnd (example: rnd 15: K21, YO). When the needle becomes too crowded, about 272 sts (34 each section), change to size 9 60" circular needle. Cont in sunset-spiral patt until 480 sts (60 sts

each section) are on needle, ending with even-numbered row. Knit 1 rnd. Work 12 rows in swirl-ribbing-border patt. Using size 10 needle, BO all sts loosely in patt.

FINISHING

With size 7 needle and RS facing, PU 108 sts along neck edge. Join, pm, and work 7 rows in swirl-ribbing-border patt. Using size 9 needle, BO all sts loosely. Weave in all ends. Block using mist method (see page 77).

SHERYL'S NOTES

Make this piece even more dramatic by continuing to work the spiral pattern for several more inches. Make sure the number of stitches is divisible by six before starting the ribbing border. Purchase additional yarn.

Carefully weave in the ends and your Sunset will be completely reversible. Wear it purl side out for a slightly more textured look, as shown on page 63, or knit side out as shown on page 62 and below.

25"

17"

120"

SUPERNOVA

During a supernova explosion, the core of a star collapses to an extremely small state and the outer layers are violently blown off. Cause your own stellar explosion with this reversible celestial wrap. Everyone will want to know how it's made.

SKILL LEVEL

Easy ◼◼◻◻

FINISHED MEASUREMENTS

Width: 70"

Length: 22½"

MATERIALS

4 skeins of Ritratto from S. Charles (53% viscose, 28% mohair, 10% polyamide, 9% polyester; 50 g/1.78 oz; 198 yds) in color 64 ③

Size 8 (5 mm) needles or size required to obtain gauge

Size 11 (8 mm) needles or size required to obtain gauge

2 stitch markers

Purchased shawl pin (optional)

GAUGE

16 sts = 4" in supernova patt using sizes 8 and 11 needles

STITCH PATTERN

supernova

(Multiple of 6 + 1)

Row 1 (RS): Using larger needles, *K1, (K1, wrapping yarn twice around needle) 5 times, rep from * to last st, K1.

Row 2: Using smaller needles, *P1, (wyib sl 5 sts pw, dropping extra wraps, insert LH needle into front of same sts and K5tog tbl, do not remove from LH needle, YO, knit same 5 sts tog tbl, do not remove from LH needle, YO and knit same 5 sts tog tbl, remove from LH needle), rep from * to last st, P1.

Row 3: Using larger needles, K4, *(K1, wrapping yarn twice around needle) 5 times, K1, rep from * to last 3 sts, K3.

Row 4: Using smaller needles, P4, *(wyib sl 5 sts pw, dropping extra wraps, insert LH needle into front of same sts and K5tog tbl, do not remove from LH needle, YO, knit same 5 sts tog tbl, do not remove from LH needle, YO, knit same 5 sts tog tbl, remove from LH needle), P1, rep from * to last 3 sts, P3.

Rep rows 1–4 for patt.

SUPERNOVA

WRAP

Using smaller needles, CO 91 sts.
Knit 5 rows. Setup row: K3, pm, knit
to last 3 sts, pm, K3. Establish patt as
follows: work 3 edge sts in garter st,
sl marker, work in supernova patt to
marker, sl marker, work 3 edge sts
in garter st. Cont in established patt
until piece measures 70". Change
to smaller needles and knit 6 rows.
Using larger needles, BO all sts
loosely.

FINISHING

Weave in all ends. Block using mist
method (see page 77).

SHERYL'S NOTES

To brighten a dark-colored
winter coat, position wrap
over your shoulders and pin in
place under the coat's collar.

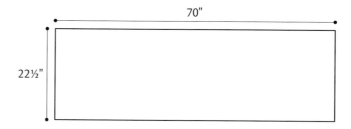

70"

22½"

TWILIGHT

Photographers and painters refer to twilight, the time between sunset and darkness and the time between night and sunrise, as the blue hour due to the romantic qualities of ambient light. In this wrap, the openness of the zigzag-trellis pattern allows the blue mohair to suffuse the richer hue of the recycled silk.

SKILL LEVEL

Intermediate ◼◼◼▢

FINISHED MEASUREMENTS

Width: 80"

Length: 20"

MATERIALS

A: 4 skeins of Recycled Silk DK from Mango Moon (100% silk; 150 yds). Each skein is unique color. **[3]**

B: 3 skeins of Kid Mohair from Mango Moon (70% mohair, 30% nylon; 175 yds) in color red. **[4]**

Size 11 (8 mm) needles or size required to obtain gauge

28 beads, 5 mm

Big-eye beading needle

Sewing thread

GAUGE

9 sts = 4" with 1 strand of A and 1 strand of B held tog in patt

STITCH PATTERN

zigzag trellis

(Even number of sts + 4)

Chart on page 70.

Rows 1, 3, 5, and 7 (RS): K2, *YO, K2tog, rep from * to last 2 sts, K2.

Row 2 and all WS rows: K2, purl to last 2 sts, K2.

Rows 9, 11, 13, and 15: K2, *ssk, YO, rep from * to last 2 sts, K2.

Row 16: K2, purl to last 2 sts, K2.

Rep rows 1–16 for patt.

WRAP

With 1 strand of A and 1 strand of B held tog, CO 46 sts. Knit 2 rows. Work setup row as follows: K2, purl to last 2 sts, K2. Work in zigzag-trellis patt until piece measures about 79", ending with row 16. Knit 2 rows. BO all sts loosely.

TWILIGHT

FINISHING

Weave in all ends. Make corner tassels as follows: With 1 strand of A and 1 strand of B held tog, cut 10 strands, each 12" long. Fold strands in half and pull folded loop through a corner st on wrap. Draw yarn ends through loop and pull to tighten. Trim ends to even them. String 7 beads on a double strand of sewing thread and knot securely to form ring just above tassel knot. Rep for each corner (make 4 tassels total).

SHERYL'S NOTES

Mango Moon supports the nongovernmental organization Nepal Women's Empowerment Group (N-WEG) to help women who have been rescued from abusive situations. The women who come to the shelter are able to use their spinning and knitting skills to rebuild their lives, while continuing to care for their children. Proceeds provide a safe shelter, health care, education, and the dignity of financial independence.

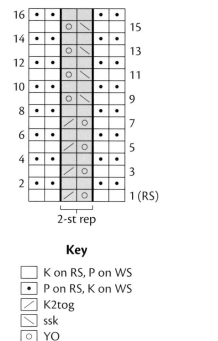

2-st rep

Key

	K on RS, P on WS
•	P on RS, K on WS
⁄	K2tog
\	ssk
○	YO

20"

80"

VINES

Fast-growing climbing vines create attractive garden displays. The repetitive lace pattern with slightly scalloped cast-on edge and baby-cable border, which does not require a cable needle, works up rapidly and is a joy to knit. The attractive ruana shape provides a striking and versatile wrap that is a joy to wear.

SKILL LEVEL

Intermediate ◼◼◼◻

FINISHED MEASUREMENTS

Back width: 39"

Front width: 16½"

Length: 30"

MATERIALS

5 skeins of Creative Focus Brushed Alpaca from Nashua Knits (100% alpaca; 50 g/1.75 oz; 190 yds) in color 799 Herbal

Size 10 (6 mm) needles or size required to obtain gauge

2 stitch markers

2 stitch holders

Purchased shawl pin (optional)

GAUGE

14 sts = 4" in vine patt

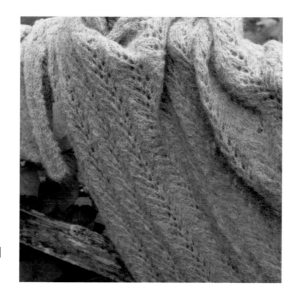

STITCH PATTERNS

baby cable

(Multiple of 4)

Chart on page 73.

Row 1 (RS): *P1, K2, P1, rep from *.

Rows 2 and 4: *K1, P2, K1, rep from *.

Row 3: *P1, K2tog and leave on LH needle, insert RH needle between 2 sts just worked and knit first st again, sl both sts from needle, P1, rep from *.

Rep rows 1–4 for patt.

vine

(Multiple of 9 + 4)

Chart on page 73.

Row 1 (RS): K3, *YO, K2, ssk, K2tog, K2, YO, K1, rep from * to last st, K1.

Rows 2 and 4: Purl.

Row 3: K2, *YO, K2, ssk, K2tog, K2, YO, K1, rep from * to last 2 sts, K2.

Rep rows 1–4 for patt.

WRAP

back

CO 138 sts. Purl 1 row. Knit 1 row. Setup row: K4, pm, K130, pm, K4. Establish patt as follows: work first 4 sts in baby-cable patt, sl marker, work 130 sts in vine patt, sl marker, work last 4 sts in baby-cable patt. Cont in established patt until piece measures 30", ending with row 3 of vine patt. Place all sts on holder.

VINES

left front

CO 57 sts. Purl 1 row. Knit 1 row. Setup row: K4, pm, K49, pm, K4. Establish patt as follows: work first 4 sts in baby-cable patt, sl marker, work 49 sts in vine patt, sl marker, work last 4 sts in baby-cable patt. Cont in established patt until piece measures 30", ending with row 4 of vine patt. Sl 53 sts on holder. Cont in baby-cable patt on 4 rem sts for 4" for back-tab neck edge. BO 4 sts.

right front

Work as for left front until piece measures 30", ending with row 4 of vine patt. Work first 4 sts in baby-cable patt for back-tab neck edge, sl rem 53 sts on holder. Work 4 sts in baby-cable patt for back-tab neck edge for 4". BO 4 sts.

FINISHING

With RS tog, and using 3-needle BO (see page 74), join front and back pieces, matching side edges. BO rem 32 sts on center back. Sew left- and right-tab edges along back neck, joining at center back. Weave in all ends. Block using mist-and-pin method (see page 77).

SHERYL'S NOTES

To make a simple rectangular wrap that's approximately 16½" wide and 60" long, follow the directions for making two fronts, eliminating the back-tab neck edge. Join using three-needle bind off.

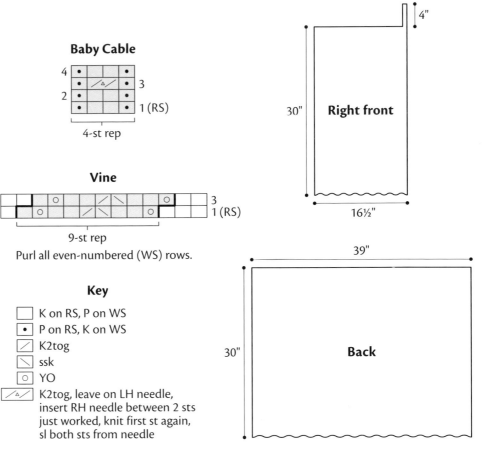

Baby Cable

4-st rep

Vine

9-st rep

Purl all even-numbered (WS) rows.

Key

☐ K on RS, P on WS
• P on RS, K on WS
╱ K2tog
╲ ssk
○ YO
K2tog, leave on LH needle, insert RH needle between 2 sts just worked, knit first st again, sl both sts from needle

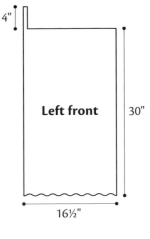

TECHNIQUES

The following are a few of the techniques used in the projects in this book.

CASTING ON

Here are two techniques I like to use when casting on in the middle of a project.

backward-loop cast on

This is an easy cast on whenever you need to add stitches within a row. *Form a loop so the end of the yarn is in front of the needle. Insert right needle into this loop and tighten gently. Repeat from * for the desired number of stitches.

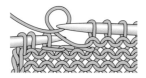

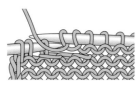

cable cast on

Make a slipknot and place on a needle. Knit into the loop and place the resulting stitch on the left needle by inserting the left needle into the stitch from the right side of the loop. *Insert the right needle between the two stitches, wrap the yarn around the needle, pull the new loop through to the front, and place it on the left needle. Repeat from * for the specified number of stitches.

GRAPHS

Some patterns have graphs associated with them that actually allow you to see the design on paper. Each square represents a stitch. Begin reading the graph at the bottom right-hand corner. Rows are numbered along the side. Odd-numbered rows are worked right to left and even-numbered rows (often the wrong-side rows) are read left to right. If there are no even-numbered rows on the graph, the pattern will tell you what to do as they are often simply purl rows. With a little practice, graphs are very easy to use and are often preferred by many knitters.

JOINING A NEW BALL OF YARN

Whenever possible, attach a new ball of yarn at the beginning of the row. Tie the new strand onto the old tail with a single knot. Slide the new knot up the old tail to the needle and begin knitting with the new yarn. Weave in the tails as you finish the project.

THREE-NEEDLE BIND OFF

Place half the stitches on one needle and half on a second needle. With right sides together, hold both needles in your left hand. Insert the right-hand needle into the first stitch on the front needle, and then into the first stitch on the back needle; knit the two stitches together at the same time. Repeat with the next two stitches on the left-hand needles; then bind off loosely in the usual manner. Continue knitting two stitches together from the front and back needles and binding off across the row. When one stitch remains on the right-hand needle, cut the tail and pass it through the last loop.

Knit 1 stitch from front needle and 1 stitch from back needle together.

Bind off.

YARN OVER (YO)

If the last stitch worked is a knit stitch, bring the yarn between the two needles to the front. Take the yarn over the right-hand needle to the back: one YO made. If the last stitch worked is a purl stitch, the yarn is already in the front. Take the yarn over the right needle to the back: one YO made.

PICKING UP STITCHES ALONG A BOUND-OFF EDGE

Begin at the right-hand corner with the right side of the work facing you and a separate ball of yarn. Insert a needle under two strands of the bound-off edge, wrap as if to knit, and pull the loop through to the right side, leaving the newly formed stitch on the needle. Continue across, picking up one stitch per bound-off stitch.

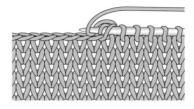

SEAMS

A few of the projects require seams to join the pieces together. There are different ways to make seams, depending on what kind of stitches you are joining.

stitches to stitches (vertical stitches to vertical stitches)

Work on the right side with wrong sides together and right sides facing out. Insert a tapestry needle threaded with matching yarn under the two strands forming the V that points toward the seam; pull the yarn through and repeat on the other side, working V to V across the seam. The seam should look like a row of knitting. Work carefully and do not pull the yarn too tight.

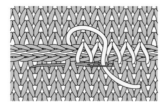

stitches to rows (vertical stitches to horizontal stitches)

Work on the right side with wrong sides together and right sides facing out. Insert a tapestry needle threaded with matching yarn under the two strands forming the V that points toward the seam, pull the yarn through, and on the other side, insert the needle under one or two bars between stitches. Repeat until the seam is complete. Because there will be more bars than Vs, you will have to alternate the number of bars worked to make a smooth, flat seam. Generally there is a three-to-four ratio, meaning that working one bar and one V three times, and then working two bars and one V across the seam, should accommodate the difference.

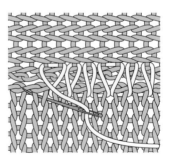

CROCHET

Some projects are finished with a crocheted edge. The stitches listed here will help you with the basics.

chain stitch (ch)

Wrap yarn around hook and pull through the loop on the hook.

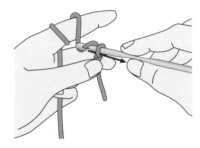

single crochet (sc)

Working from right to left with the right side facing you, insert the hook into the next stitch, yarn over the hook, pull the loop to the front, yarn over the hook, and pull the loop through both loops on the hook. Space stitches so the edge lies flat.

Insert hook into stitch, yarn over hook, pull loop to the front, yarn over hook.

Pull loop through both loops on hook.

The formula for spacing stitches on a vertical edge is to work into each knot at the edge. For a horizontal row, the formula is one crochet stitch for every one and one-half knit stitches. However, even using the formula as a guide, it may be necessary to skip or add stitches to keep the edge flat.

When working a crochet edge on a knitted piece, always begin by working a row of single crochet to stabilize the edges. To work additional rows of single crochet, insert the hook under both loops of the stitch below, and then work one single crochet into each stitch in the previous row.

double crochet (dc)

Working from right to left with the right side facing you, yarn over the hook, insert the hook into the next stitch, yarn over the hook, and pull the loop to the front (three loops on hook). Yarn over the hook and pull through the first two loops on the hook (two loops remain on hook).

Yarn over the hook and pull through the remaining two loops (one loop remains on hook).

Yarn over hook, insert hook into stitch, yarn over hook, pull through to front.

Yarn over hook, pull through two loops on hook.

Yarn over hook, pull through remaining two loops on hook.

BLOCKING

First choose a flat, waterproof surface to spread out the piece to be blocked. Blocking boards can be purchased, the top of an ironing board works for smaller pieces, or the floor covered with a towel will work. Regardless of the method used for blocking, the piece should remain in place until dry.

damp-towel method

Lay the knit piece on the surface, shaping to specified dimensions. Dampen a towel that's large enough to cover the knitted piece. Running a saturated towel through the spin cycle of the washing machine works well. Place the damp towel over the knitted piece and leave it for one to two hours. Remove the towel, but let the piece dry completely before moving it.

mist method

Lay the knitted piece on the surface, shaping to specified dimensions. Fill a clean spray bottle with water, mist the piece lightly, and allow to dry completely before moving.

mist-and-pin method

Lay the knitted piece on the surface and pin to specified measurements. Fill a clean spray bottle with water and mist the piece heavily. Allow to dry completely before removing the pins.

wet method

Dip the knitted piece in cool water. Gently squeeze out the water. *Do not wring or twist.* Roll the piece in an absorbent bath towel to blot out the excess water. Spread out on the surface and pin to the specified dimensions. Allow to dry completely before removing the pins.

ABBREVIATIONS AND GLOSSARY

beg	begin(ning)
BO	bind off
ch	chain
cn	cable needle
CO	cast on
cont	continue
dc	double crochet
dec	decrease
dpn	double-pointed needle(s)
EOR	every other row
g	gram(s)
inc	increase
K	knit
K1B	Knit into the stitch on the row below
K1f&b	Knit into the front and back of the next stitch
K1, P1 ribbing	Knit 1, purl 1. On other side, knit the knit stitches and purl the purl stitches as they face you
K2tog	Knit 2 stitches together
K3tog	Knit 3 stitches together
kw	knitwise
LH	left hand

m	meter(s)
M1	Make 1 stitch
M1R	Make 1 stitch slanted to the right (see page 59)
M1L	Make 1 stitch slanted to the left (see page 59)
oz	ounce(s)
P	purl
P1f&b	Purl into the front and back of the next stitch
patt	pattern
pm	place marker
psso	Pass slipped stitch over
p2sso	Pass 2 slipped stitches over
P2tog	Purl 2 stitches together
P2tog tbl	Purl 2 stitches together through the back loop
P3tog	Purl 3 stitches together
PU	pick up and knit
pw	purlwise
rem	remain(ing)
RH	right hand
rnd(s)	round(s)
RS	right side
sc	single crochet

sl	slip
sl 2 kw-K1-p2sso	Slip 2 stitches together as if to knit, knit 1 stitch, pass the 2 slipped stitches over the knit stitch
sl 1 K2tog-psso	Slip 1 stitch as if to knit, knit 2 stitches together, pass the slipped stitch over the knit stitch
sl st	slip stitch
ssk	slip 2 stitches knitwise, 1 at a time, to right needle, then insert left needle from left to right into front loops and knit 2 stitches together
st(s)	stitch(es)
St st	stockinette stitch (Knit 1 row, then purl 1 row back; knit every row in the round.)
tbl	through the back loop
tog	together
WS	wrong side
wyib	with yarn in back
wyif	with yarn in front
yd(s)	yard(s)
YO	yarn over

USEFUL INFORMATION

STANDARD YARN WEIGHTS							
Yarn-Weight Symbol and Category Name	**0** Lace	**1** Super Fine	**2** Fine	**3** Light	**4** Medium	**5** Bulky	**6** Super Bulky
Types of Yarn in Category	Fingering, 10-count crochet thread	Sock, Fingering, Baby	Sport, Baby	DK, Light worsted	Worsted, Afghan, Aran	Chunky, Craft, Rug	Bulky, Roving
Knit Gauge Range* in Stockinette Stitch to 4"	33 to 40** sts	27 to 32 sts	23 to 26 sts	21 to 24 sts	16 to 20 sts	12 to 15 sts	6 to 11 sts
Recommended Needle in Metric Size Range	1.5 to 2.25 mm	2.25 to 3.25 mm	3.25 to 3.75 mm	3.75 to 4.5 mm	4.5 to 5.5 mm	5.5 to 8 mm	8 mm and larger
Recommended Needle in U.S. Size Range	000 to 1	1 to 3	3 to 5	5 to 7	7 to 9	9 to 11	11 and larger

*These are guidelines only. The above ranges reflect the most commonly used gauges and needle or hook sizes for specific yarn categories.

**Lace-weight yarns are usually knit or crocheted on larger needles and hooks to create lacy, openwork patterns. Accordingly, a gauge range is difficult to determine. Always follow the gauge stated in your pattern.

METRIC CONVERSION CHART				
m	=	yds	x	0.9144
yds	=	m	x	1.0936
g	=	oz	x	28.35
oz	=	g	x	0.0352

RESOURCES

AslanTrends USA
www.aslantrends.com
Artesanal

Berroco Yarns
www.berroco.com
Bonsai
Palace

Claudia Hand Painted Yarns
www.claudiaco.com
Fingering

Colinette
www.colinette.com
Jitterbug

Debbie Bliss
www.knittingfever.com
Donegal *Luxury Tweed*

Filatura Di Crosa
www.tahkistacycharles.com
Superior

Green Mountain Spinnery
www.spinnery.com
Green Mountain Green

Lorna's Laces
www.lornaslaces.net
Lion and Lamb

Louet North America
www.louet.com
Euroflax
Mooi

Malabrigo Yarn
www.malabrigoyarn.com
Lace

Mango Moon Yarns
www.mangomoonyarns.com
Recycled Silk DK
Mohair

Manos del Uruguay
www.fairmountfibers.com
Manos Silk Blend

Nashua Knits
www.nashuaknits.com
Creative Focus Brushed Alpaca

Plymouth Yarns
www.plymouthyarn.com
Royal Llama Silk

Rowan Yarns
www.westminsterfibers.com
Pure Silk DK

S. Charles
www.tahkistacycharles.com
Karma
Ritratto

Universal Yarn
www.universalyarn.com
Aster Magic